The 18,000KM Diaries

China To The UK Via The North Cape To Save Sight

Sir Nicholas White, Bt.

Ellie White®
Gloucestershire

Copyright

Ellie White
10 Shipton Moyne
Tetbury
Gloucestershire
GL8 8PP

www.elliewhite.co.uk

FIRST EDITION

First published by Ellie White in March 2022.

A catalogue record for this book is available from the British Library.

ISBN: 978-1-909972-18-6

Typesetting and design by White Media.
www.whitemedia.uk

In Loving Memory of Sue

Acknowledgements

I would like to thank the following Companies and individuals who helped and encouraged me in the preparation and reporting on my progress throughout my journey.

Omnia Dubai – Toby Jordan, who posted a weekly diary through Gulf News of my progress.

China International Travel Services, which organised my seven guides and arranged hotel accommodation throughout China. The guides were all young enough to be my children, spoke reasonable English and saw parts of the country that they had never seen before. They were driven by me, in comfort, able to see the sights, rather than having to give a running-commentary to guests on a bus.

Rudi Jagersbacher, who I had originally met back in 1984, who was the President of Hilton Hotels for the Middle East and Africa. Rudi kindly gave a reception at the Hilton on the Creek, Dubai, on my return to Dubai to hand back my Dubai number plate. The reception followed a visit to the Orbis Flying Eye Hospital at Dubai Airport and he invited all the Orbis staff to join us.

Shauket, my guide through Uzbekistan, whose knowledge of his country was exceptional and whose company I much enjoyed.

Dan, my guide through western Kazakhstan and to Moscow, as without his ability to speak Russian, I think that I could have ended up in trouble with the Police.

My deep gratitude to Omar Ashur and Saeed El Halal and the owner of Future Pipe Group, Fouad Makhzoumi, who if he had not employed me for 12 years, based in Dubai, the trip would never have occurred. I also would not have visited China and met both Jushi and CPIC, who were so generous in their support of Orbis, The Flying Eye Hospital.

Finally, my thanks to SightSavers International and Orbis for everything that they, through their volunteers, do for the thousands of people that they have helped to be able to see. May their wonderful work continue.

Contents

Chapter 1

Preparations In The United Arab Emirates

This book is aimed at sharing a unique experience of a journey that I undertook in the summer of 2006 by describing the planning, places visited through photographs as well as anecdotal episodes that occurred whilst travelling.

The story began towards the end of 2004 when I decided that I should consider retiring from Dubai as at that time I had worked there for 10 years, Sue, my wife had died two and a half years before from a brain tumour and my three children, Christopher, Simon and Annabelle were all living in England and I only saw them at Christmas or for two weeks in the summer when I would take some leave.

I had worked for a fascinating Lebanese company called The Future Pipe Group and had seen it develop from a single factory in Dubai to one that had 11 factories around the world, majority of which were located in the Middle East. Future Pipe manufactured Glass Reinforced Pipes and Epoxy pipes for the Water, Sewage and Oil related markets. In my 12 years (1994 – 2006) I had seen Dubai grow from being a town with a total population of 750,000 people to one of over 3 million, the two pictures show how in just 14 years there had been such development.

I read a quotation from the Ruler of Dubai, H.H. Sheikh Mohammed Al Maktoum which again gave me encouragement, especially as I had seen Dubai grow over my 12 years there.

Most people talk - We do things
They plan - We achieve
They hesitate - We move ahead
We are a living proof that when human beings have the courage and commitment to transform a dream in to reality there is nothing that can stop them - Dubai is a living example of that.

1991
Dubai's Sheikh Zayed Road viewed from the top of the World Trade Centre

2005
Dubai's Sheikh Zayed Road viewed from the top of the World Trade Centre

I decided that if I was to return home I should undertake a unique and solo road journey that would cross China back to the UK via Nord Cap, the most northerly point in Europe, and probably that would not have been undertaken by anyone else as this was likely to be the last occasion that I would have for such an opportunity. You might ask 'why go solo' and the answer to that was that you can travel as far as you want on any day and although it may sound very selfish you will see what you want and are indirectly forced to talk to the local people.

I went to Magrudy's bookstall in the City Centre in Dubai and bought, for £100.00, *The Times Atlas of the World* and then sat down in my apartment to work out a route home. I asked myself was it possible to re-trace a drive that I had undertaken in 1968, when I had completed a four year assignment with the Courage Brewery Group in East Africa. On that occasion I took my VW Beetle from Mombassa in Kenya to Karachi in Pakistan. From there I drove up through Pakistan, over the Khyber Pass to Kabul and through Afghanistan. From there, the route took me into Iran and then a right-turn into Armenia, which was then part of the Soviet Union. Across Georgia I went, up to Moscow, St. Petersburg and from there crossed in to Finland and drove up over the Arctic Circle into Norway, down the Coast to Bergen and back to Newcastle by ferry for the final drive home to Wateringbury in Kent. The journey took 9 weeks and covered 9,500 miles against an estimate of 9,000 miles.

That journey could not be repeated today due to the problems in Afghanistan, difficulties in taking one's own vehicle through Iran and the terrorist threats through the Southern Caucuses countries. The only option therefore was to travel further North. Then the route suddenly fell in to place in my mind, as since I was aged about 10 I had always wanted to visit Tibet and Lhasa, but would I ever obtain approval to travel there in my own car? The starting point therefore had to be Shanghai!

With a piece of paper and pencil I traced the road to measure the distances to be covered and the towns to be visited *en route* and found the distance would be 18,000 miles, especially if I was to re-trace a section of my 1968 route through Russia and Scandinavia. The time that it would take to travel the route I estimated would be 100 – 120 days. I was not in a hurry and I wanted to ensure that I had enough time to undertake a certain amount of sightseeing.

I went home for Christmas, but did not mention anything about the journey. I was asked by the children before I left Dubai what I would like as a Christmas present and much to their surprise I actually had a suggestion, which was a digital camera with a good zoom. I was asked "why, because you do not normally take photographs?", but managed to fob off an acceptable response without revealing the real answer.

The next question to be answered was when would the journey start, as the weather would be a major factor due to the snow melting and roads being impassable either in Tibet or over the Arctic Circle. So, the decision was taken that it should commence in late April ... but first I would require all the Visas and I had no idea as to whether these would be forthcoming.

I decided that I should not approach the Chinese Embassy in Dubai directly, as I considered that I would be given an out of hand negative answer. So, I wrote a rather over the top letter stating what I wanted to do, the route that I would like to travel and addressed the letter direct to the President of The Peoples Republic of China, Mr. Hu Jintao. The letter was delivered to the Chinese Embassy in Dubai as I had no idea of an address in Beijing. (The letter and responses are in appendix 1).

After six weeks I had received no response, so I telephoned the Chinese Ambassador and spoke to his secretary, who remembered my letter and admitted that they had opened it before sending it on to Beijing. He said that as yet no response had been received, but he would follow the matter up. Ten days later I received a call from the Ambassador's Secretary to say a response was on its way and that the letter had been sent to the Ministry of Foreign Affairs and then forwarded on to Ministry of Culture and Tourism.

A week later I had still not received a response, so I made another call and this time he apologised that he had been away and would I send a driver down to collect the letter. On receiving it I opened it with trepidation and to my utter elation, pleasure and surprise the answer was approval in principle subject to two provisions:

1. At all times I must have a guide
2. All accommodation must be booked through a Chinese Tourist Company.

The letter was signed by the Deputy Minister and she gave me the name and telephone number of her Assistant, who spoke English and would be able to help me.

The outlined approval was received in early June, which meant that the trip could not start until 2006, as there was still a lot of planning and approvals required. In the meanwhile over the space of a few months Christopher, Annabelle and lastly Simon announced that they were each engaged, so I definitely needed to work for another year as all three would be married within the space of 11 months!

Left:
The map created by my son, Christopher, to outline the planned route of the trip. The map was used for publicity purposes to raise awareness of the project

I asked Omnia, a Dubai branding and digital agency, if they would be prepared to write a programme that would record my journey and put the whole progress live on the Internet. They agreed and prepared everything - but with one error, which I did not pick up on - they had replaced miles for kilometers, The title of the trip became "18,000km to Save Sight, Shanghai to London via The North Cape".

I decided that I would tell no one about the journey until I had all the details sorted out, as I did not want rumours running around.

I contacted Mr. Li Mingxing, the Chinese Deputy Minister's Assistant, who put me in touch with a Mr. Baoquan of the Chinese International Tourist Company. As it turned out, he worked in the German section, but luckily spoke some English. I sent him my route plan and requested him to obtain the necessary approvals. At the outset he could not understand that I would be driving my own car and recommended that I should fly between places, especially to Lhasa. He eventually understood my plan, but came back and said I could not and would not be given permission to drive from Lhasa along the Himalayas to Kashgar as the road was too high and dangerous in places. He suggested that having visited Lhasa I should drive due North over the Tibetan Plateau and join the Silk Road in Dunhuang and from there follow the Silk Road around to the Kazakh border. He then came back and said that from Chengdu I must take a different road to Lhasa from that which I had planned and that this would be the same as the one going to Dunhuang. So I said "no this would defeat the object of trying to see as much of the country as I could, I want to travel South West from Chengdu to the Tibetan Border and then on to Lhasa." He initially came back and said that I could not, but I was not going to give up! Being firmly insistent they eventually relented and agreed, but said that the road was dangerous and not in good condition.

Once the initial approval was obtained to travel through China I approached the Kazakh Ministry of Tourism, but could find no-one who spoke English and so reverted to the Kazakh Embassy in Dubai. Here I met a lovely man Mr. Najhmedin, First Secretary, who initially said this was impossible as people do not drive their cars across Kazakhstan. However, after a number of meetings we became good friends and he could not help me enough, although he continued to say that he could not guarantee me approval and could only try his best by writing to the Ministry of Tourism.

The Uzbekistan Embassy said that there was no problem in getting a Visa, but they did not know about transiting a car, so I contacted Asia Travel in Tashkent who could not have been more helpful. They said there was absolutely no problem and they would arrange for a guide to be at the border at the time and day that I was due to cross from Kazakhstan. I decided that I needed a guide for my week in Uzbekistan, as otherwise I would not understand the history and see the important sites.

The Russian Embassy put me in touch with their Travel Agent in Dubai and said there should be no difficulty. So approval seemed alright, except for Kazakhstan. I decided to press on regardless with the detailed plans.

The next major decision to be taken was what vehicle should I ideally use? I would like a Volkswagen Tuareg (4x4) that I would buy and take delivery of in Shanghai - provided the vehicle met the European and British Standards, as the VW Beetle had served me exceptionally well in 1968 when I undertook my previous journey. I wrote to the President of Volkswagen and my letter was passed on to the Head of Public Relations, who in turn passed me on to the Head of their Joint Venture in China. After many follow-ups, that was the last I heard from Volkswagen. I then turned my attention to Toyota, but they said that the vehicles delivered to China would not conform to European standards, so that ended that line. Nissan found the whole matter too difficult and said they could not help. On my last trip to Nissan I was walking down the Airport Road in Dubai and walked by the Volvo showroom. Much to my surprise I saw they had a 4x4, as I was not aware they built one.

I went in and spoke to the Salesman who said all Volvos are built in Gothenburg in Sweden and therefore conform to European Specifications. The Muslim Holy Month of Ramadan had just started and consequently all vehicles purchased during this period were subject to a 25% discount! So I ordered a Volvo XC90 Turbo 2.5, Ruby Red that would be shipped from Sweden and arrive in Dubai in the 2nd/3rd week of January 2006. I decided to have the Ruby Red colour as a safety precaution, as the majority of vehicles are Silver or Cream in Kazakhstan and Russia and so I considered it might be wiser to have a vehicle that stood out, especially against high-jacking.

On the 8th / 9th October 2005 whilst changing in my apartment before going out to dinner, I was watching a BBC World programme that was narrated by Sir John Major on the work of SightSavers International in India. This programme so intrigued me that I decided that there and then I must add a Charity purpose and objective to my journey. I contacted SightSavers to see whether they were involved in various countries that I had had involvement with during my lifetime. They could not fulfil all my requirements, should I be successful in raising some sizable amount of money. My request was that the money raised should go to the following countries, namely:

- Nepal, because I had been a Gurkha Officer and also had recruited ex-Gurkhas and other Nepalese to work in Future Pipe Group's factories in Dubai and the Gulf area.
- Kenya and Tanzania as I had worked there from 1964 – 1968 with the Courage Group
- India, Pakistan as most of our Employees in the Middle East came from these countries

Below:
ORBIS's Flying Eye Hospital aircraft, which was donated to ORBIS by Fed-Ex and fitted out as a hospital by Alcon.

- China because without their approval the journey would never have commenced and I had visited China from Dubai on four occasions, buying fibreglass for the Future Pipe Group, for whom I worked.

SightSavers predominantly work in partnership with Commonwealth Countries, but there was another Charity, Orbis UK, who did exactly the same, but all around the Developing World. When I came home for Christmas I met up with both SightSavers and Orbis and they were both supportive of my plans. I set myself a stretching target of a £500,000 that I hoped I would be able to raise through of my business contacts and friends.

I was most impressed by Orbis as they explained that they have a Flying Eye Hospital that has been donated by Fed-Ex and fitted out as a specialist Eye hospital by Alcon. This aeroplane flies at the invitation of the country to be visited and airport fees are free. Usually, over a two week period, volunteer surgeons, anaesthetists and nurses undertake operations, with local surgeons being instructed in the details of the operation, whilst in the back of the aeroplane doctors and nurses watch live operations being undertaken via 17 micro cameras, all being talked through by the volunteer surgeon. A very clever way of teaching and involving the local partner hospital's staff. The cost of operating the aeroplane does not take any of the Orbis donated monies.

Both Charities told me that there are some 37 million people who are blind, predominantly in the Developing World and of these 29 million should not be, if there was proper eye-care available. 18 million suffer from cataracts. The charities work at the invitation of the Governments concerned, with local hospitals or clinics to transfer their knowledge, by teaching Doctors to perform ophthalmic operations, train Nurses and Community Workers to undertake eye/sight awareness courses and eye checks, as well as providing the sophisticated equipment required. For a mere £17.00, a person can have a 15 - 20 minutes operation that can restore in most cases their ability to see. Horrifyingly, every 5 minutes one child goes blind some where in the world and of these 50% are dead within two years, as they are cast out by their families because they are of no long-term benefit to the family and community. The cost for a child is £25.00 to be given its sight back, but must be operated on within five years of going blind. This small amount of money not only helps the blind individual to become self sufficient once again - or maybe for the first time in their life - but also relieves the family and local community of the stresses and burden of caring for a blind person.

In late December 2005 Mr. Baoquan of CITS informed me that he was transferring to Germany and that Mr. Li Yue would take over my file. Within two weeks Mr. Yue informed me that nothing had been done in obtaining all the approvals from the Provincial Governments, Police and Army. I informed him that he therefore had to get down to it quickly, as time was beginning to run away and the journey was shortly due to start. He came back and said he had never done something like this before and could not guarantee a result, so I contacted Mr. Li Mingxing in the Ministry of Tourism. He told me not to worry and that everything would be sorted out. I left to the UK for Christmas.

On the 17th December all my children were at home, as on the following day my first Grandson Archie was to be christened. As we sat down to dinner I broke the news to them about my forthcoming trip. Christopher said "Dad can I come with you", Annabelle said "good on you, go and do it", Simon said nothing he being the more cautious one but a week later for Christmas he had bought me three books on the Silk Road and a map which were very useful for the more detailed preparation and understanding of the history and places that I would visit.

In January I applied for my Chinese Visa. At first I received a 30 day Visa, which had to be changed, as it had been agreed that travelling across China and Tibet would take 42 days. Consequently, they gave me a 60 day Visa, which is most unusual. The Kazakhs said that I needed to have both the Chinese and Russian Visas in my passport before they would consider my application. The Russian and Uzbek Visas were received with no difficulty, but it was not until the 18th April, two days before I was due to fly to Shanghai, that I finally received the Kazakh Visa. There was some serious nail biting!

On the 20th January I took delivery of my Ruby Red Volvo XC90 and so had a chance to become accustomed to it in Dubai, before it was due to be shipped to Shanghai in a container on the 30th March. I

Above:
My new Volvo XC90 D5 in front of the Royal Mirage Hotel, Dubai

asked the Volvo Distributor, Al Futtaim Motors, if I could go to their workshops in the evening to learn about the engine, which is what I had done with VW in 1968 for the Beetle, but they said no as the car is completely computerised. I then asked them what spares I should take, other than two extra wheels, as the supplied spare is only one of the 80km/h tyres which would be of no use. They said some bulbs, perhaps a fan belt, oil, gearbox and brake fluid. The spare wheels they gave me for free, as most Arabs want the low profile tyres and so they had many regular tyres spare. In addition I bought two twenty litre fuel cans and tow ropes. I decide everything must fit inside the vehicle as a roof rack could cause unnecessary risks and problems.

Bob Collier of Al Futtaim Exel agreed to ship the car in a container for free from Dubai to Shanghai. He admitted later that the cost of a container was $15.00 as China desperately needed every container they could lay their hands on and he would arrange for their

Chinese partners to clear the car through Customs, but I would have to pick up the local costs.

Then I had to obtain Car Insurance Cover, but no company would underwrite it, except for in Europe. I would have to buy insurance in each country *en route* - a potential problem. I also would have to obtain a Carnet de Passage as I was going to drive on the UAE registration plates. I went to the Automobile Association of Dubai, which luckily was adjacent to my apartment. Needless to say, they had never before been requested for any of these countries, except Europe. I had to pay a £10,000.00 deposit which I could only get back after I returned the registration plates to Dubai and even then, only if each country had stamped the entry and exit on the relevant page – a concern as when studying the back of the document it did not appear any of these countries recognized the document.

The preparations were complete and it was time to bid farewell to all my colleagues in Future Pipe and friends in Dubai. There appeared to be a non-stop round of parties. As a parting gift, Future Pipe, through the Group Financial Vice President, Omar Ashur, invited me to a presentation where most of the Gulf Eternit employees were present and he presented me with the latest Toshiba lap-top which had been fully set up by my great friend and IT Manager, Saeed El Halal.

The car was handed over to the shippers three weeks before I was due to fly out so that it would arrive the day before I was due to land in Shanghai on the 20th April.

Below:
Dr. Omar Ashur presenting me with a farewell gift.

Chapter 2

China and Tibet

April 20th 2006

At 02.15 am I took off from Dubai and arrived in Shanghai at 14.55pm after a comfortable flight. Luckily I was in the front row of the Economy Class. Went through Passport quickly, but it took an hour to collect my cases.

Was met by Max, my guide for the leg from Shanghai to Yichang. Max is 35 and married to Ma Ling Xiao, an Attorney at Law. He was originally a teacher and for the last three years has been a guide.

He is a very pleasant, cheerful person, who is amazed by the forthcoming trip and looking forward to it as he has never had such a tour before. He is very much involved with arranging the clearance of the car and has had to visit Customs for me. Customs had trouble in fully understanding the Carnet de Passage as the car has additional items such as the 2 empty fuel tanks, an oxygen set for the high altitude, spare wheels etc.. I had to take copies of the letters to Mr. Hu Jintao and the reply from the Ministry of Tourism as the Chinese are very hierarchical and these letters pull weight.

Had an early dinner and went to bed by 10.00pm.

April 21st 2006

Alarm went off at 07.00am, had breakfast and then went for a walk along the Bund, which is the old Western style waterfront along the Huang Pu River, which is really picturesque. On the other side of the river is the Financial Centre with the International Convention Tower, called the Oriental Pearl TV Tower. The river is very busy with barges and ships continuously ploughing up and down the river, many of them filled to the gunnels.

The Bund is crowded with tourists, both Chinese and Foreign with many peddlers of nick-nacks, postcards etc. The azaleas were in full bloom and all the leaves out.

In the evening I met up with Customs in the Hotel to discuss the clearance of the car. It had been agreed that I could drive on my International Driving Licence and that the car can go on UAE plates.

Above:
The Bund, Shanghai.

April 22nd 2006

Walked down the Bund again and then on to the Yu Yuan Gardens and old town. The Yu Yuan Gardens are 400 years old and divided up in to 40 sections, separated by buildings or walls. The wood carvings are very impressive especially those on the roofs of all buildings, such as Dragons etc.. There is a lot of water and small curving bridges the ponds are filled with golden carp and with weeping willows and other trees surrounding.

The Yu Yuan old town is tightly packed by buildings with the traditional curved Chinese roofs and the buildings, in turn, are packed with people, as is the 9 curve bridge leading to the Yu Yuan Gardens. You get nicely hassled by staff from the shops trying to persuade you to go into their shops.

In the evening I took Max and Ma Ling out to dinner close to the hotel. The dinner was excellent. In China dinner normally starts at 6.00pm, you are not in a hurry and alcohol is consumed. On this evening it was beer, but not enormous quantities. After dinner I went in to the bar in the Hotel, which turned out to be a Karaoke bar. Some of the customers had very good voices and some dreadful with lots of warbles. It was after some-time that I realised they still had their Christmas decorations up - on the main doors there were two Father Christmas posters!

I saw that my website that had been designed in Dubai was up and running.

Below:
An old street in Yu Yuan.

Above:
The Yu Yuan Garden.

23rd April 2006

Sunday. No work other than on the building sites, so everyone was out and about on sight seeing and shopping trips, the crowds down Nanjing Road a pedestrian area was incredible. Wave upon wave of humanity. Rubbish is not dropped, but placed in the bins provided. At night it is fully flood lit like Las Vegas or Piccadilly Circus.

I walked miles and got lost on two occasions as my sense of direction took me the wrong way. I probably walked about 10 miles during the day. Went to the Jade Buddha Temple, a very much working temple where the local Chinese go to pray. The Temple dates back to 1882 when a Buddhist Monk brought two Jade statues back from Thailand. The Sitting Buddha is not allowed to be photographed, but the Reclining Buddha I was able to. The Monks are in their Yellow golden robes. In the Main Court Yard there was a cauldron burning, from which the worshippers lit their Joss Sticks and then bow to the

Above:
The reclining Jade Buddha.

four points of the Compass. From there they go to three different buildings where they pray to various deities, some of which are very garish before going on to the seated Buddha.

From there I walked back down to the Nanjing Road, had lunch and excellent chicken Caesar Salad just outside of the Ritz Carlton Hotel. In the evening I went to the Acrobatic Performance, which was stunning, very well organized and some of the acts were incredible in their feats of balance. Went to bed at 11.30pm having uploaded the photographs to my computer.

Above:
The Sunday crowd walking down Nanjing Street in Shanghai.

24th April 2006

Hoped to get car, but to no avail. A wasted day visiting various Ministries.

In the evening I met up with Jack Kuang and a colleague of his from Orbis. Jack explained about Orbis's work and that the West of China is the worst area for blindness. Orbis have undertaken quite a few projects of training Doctors and Nurses and supplying the necessary equipment to local clinics. They want to wave me off on the journey.

At the same time I had two interviews with the Shanghai Daily and the Shanghai Chinese paper about my forthcoming trip.

25th April 2006

Firstly went to get the insurance for the car which for a year cost RMB 21, 875 but will get RMB 12,400 back in a week but still very expensive. Then had to go to the Police to get a Chinese Driving

Above:
Jack Kwang and colleague from Orbis China.

Licence although originally was told that the International Licence would be ok. A fairly long-winded procedure which ended up with my having to take an exam on the Highway Code 100 questions, I managed to get 92% pass which was not bad especially as I had never seen two of the signs before which were in Chinese, then went to Customs to be told that the person who has to check the car engine and chassis number was unavailable, great apologies from Ms Hou from Customs who is working very hard but even she appears not to be able to break through the bureaucracy.

In the evening had my picture taken by the Chinese speaking newspaper. An article was in the Shanghai Daily with photo but with many inaccuracies, it stated that I was an Engineer and they did not declare where I was going to end up at the end of the journey.

26th April 2006

Another frustrating day waiting for the car, so I went to a silk exhibition to see how silk is made.

Miss Hou finally cleared the car in mid afternoon but on the way to delivering the car she had an accident which ended up that the car had to be inspected by the Shippers Insurance Company, which could not occur until the next day.

Right:
8 cocoons at the bottom of the machine being pulled to make a silk thread. A normal cocoon will pull out to 1 mile.

27th April 2006

Finally got the car at 1.00 pm but it had a long scratch all the way down the right hand side as well as a dent on the wing by the bonnet. Insurance Company agreed to pay for the repair. Then I had to go to the Police Station to get a temporary Chinese licence plate, probably the most efficient department, the number plate was in red writing and the number 00033.

Finally left Shanghai at 4.30 pm and went straight to Tongxiang where we were met by Michael of the Jushi Group, stayed at the New

Above:
Orbis girls wishing Max and me farewell at the start of the journey.

Century Hotel, had dinner there and was joined by Daniel He the Jushi International Marketing and Sales Manager. Good dinner.

28th April 2006

Checked out of the Hotel at 7.00am and went to Jushi for breakfast with Mr. Zhang, President of Jushi. We had excellent noodles, vegetables and fish.

I had visited the Jushi Group in Tongxiang on 4 previous occasions when I was buying fibreglass for the Future Pipe Group. Jushi today is the largest Fiberglass producer in the World and their quality has become fully internationally accredited.

8.00am went up to the Board Room and had a discussion about Jushi's business and my trip. At 8.30 we were joined by the Deputy Mayor of Tongxiang for a further very friendly discussion. Went down to the Entrance of the Offices where all the Senior Managers were and

Above:
Mr. Zhang Yauqiun, President of the Jushi Group presenting me a cheque for RMB200,000 ($25,000) and Mr. Xing Haihua, Vice Mayor of Tongxiang Town.

Mr. Zhang very kindly presented me with a cheque for RMB 200,000.00 (US$ 25,000) for Orbis China.

Left Tongxiang at 9.00am and drove straight through to Wuhan a distance of 908 km. The Road was good, virtually all motorway. We drove through farmland the whole way, initially past Oil Seed Rape, Rice Paddies and mulberry trees for the silk worms and on through the area of Hangzhou. From Hangzhou we drove to ZhinDeshen, which is famous for the making the fine Chinese porcelain and went to an old factory, which was more of a museum.

From there we drove to JiuJiang where Jushi has another factory. We were entertained to an excellent dinner in a restaurant, as we arrived at 6.00pm. At 7.30pm we set off to Wuhan and arrived there at 11.30pm. That last stretch was all after dark and it is at night that the main heavy lorries are allowed to travel, as otherwise the roads could not cope with the volume of traffic. The journey was not as fast, as much of the road was being repaired. This reduced the road to single lane. I was grateful for getting into bed.

Stayed at the Holiday Inn Plaza, which was very comfortable

Above:
A lady hand-painting a vase in Jiujuang.

and overlooked the Yangtse. In the morning one saw all the freighters sailing up and down the river; a hive of activity.

29th April 2006

First went to the Qingchuan Pavilion, which overlooks the Yangtse. This dates back over 200 years and here met a reporter from the Hubei TV and was interviewed on 'Live Today'.

We drove to Yitchang, 456 km away, on a good road, once again, passing through paddy fields and Oil Seed rape and wheat fields. The soil looked brilliant and I gather they can take three crops a year from the land. We stayed at the Taolualing Hotel and there met up with my new Guide, Wong, a 26 year old. He introduced me to another reporter and an article was to be printed on the 1st May. Without a doubt the trip is creating interest! Max was to leave early morning, going back to Shanghai by train.

Above:
The reporter from Hubei TV outside the Qingchuan Pavillion of the Yitang museum.

30th April 2006

Up at 6.00am to go to the Three Gorges Dam at 7.00am. I was not allowed to drive, as this is a military area and so had to take a hired car and driver. From Yichang to Three Gorges Dam takes 40 minutes through tunnels dug through the mountains. Once through the mountains you come on to a tributary of the Yangtse and eventually arrive at the river itself and to the Dam.

The Three Gorges Dam has been made in to a tourist location with Tourist Buses and well laid out gardens, models etc.. The Dam itself is enormous - 175 meters high. On the south side there will be 12 Electricity Turbines, whilst in the middle is the spillway, which in the rainy season allows the excess water to flow through three opened sluices which are spaced at the top, middle and low down on the dam wall. The purpose of this is to wash out the silt that builds up during the dry season on the upside of the dam. On the North side there are 14 electricity turbines that are working, each turbine produces 700,000 kW.

In order to allow ships to pass through, there are two sets of

locks, each with 5 locks to raise or lower the ships to go up or down stream. To pass through the complete set takes five hours. By 2007 there will be a hoist that will take smaller vessels up or down in 45 minutes.

On the way back to the Hotel we stopped at a shop that makes embroidery. The quality of the embroidery was excellent and most colourful. The girls work for five hours a day and I am sure that cannot be good for their eyes.

At the Hotel the reporter from the previous night was there to take a photograph, as there will be a front page article with picture on the 1st May *Three Gorges Daily*.

The journey from Yitang to Enshi was most interesting as it was through the mountains and the road in many places was very steep as well as the road badly breaking up in many places. The road was two way and with many heavy lorries, some overloaded, and hundreds of buses and these all had to be overtaken. I was fortunate as the Car has good overtaking pickup speed especially as the road twisted and turned in some places every 100 yards.

Arrived in Enshi and stayed at the Enshi Asia Hotel.

Above:
Looking out over the Three Gorges Dam, where there were 14 turbines working with another 12 to be completed.

Opposite page:
The 5 step locks of the Three Gorges Dam to raise ships up the 185 metres to the new river level.

Left:
The stepped fields on the road from Yitang to Enshi.

Left:
Overlooking paddy fields lying about 1000 feet below the road to Enshi.

1st May 2006

We first went to the Enshi Chieftain Castle which was built in the 1600s. It is well preserved with a Bell Tower that sits on top of a hill and from there you can see that the whole site is surrounded by a Stone wall. There are two small towers that sit either side of a valley with a rope bridge suspended between the two and then a nine tier palace. If the palace was attacked, the defenders could drop one end of the rope bridge.

The road to Wanzhou was not quite as bad as the previous day, but had more spectacular scenery. In places the road was in poor condition, chiefly due to falling rocks from the vertical hills that one wound ones way through. The farmland all looked very rich, a lot of paddy fields, fruit trees from peaches to oranges. We stayed at the Wanzhou International Hotel which was not well organized.

Below:
Looking at the Chieftain's fort at Enshi with the suspension bridge that could be lowered, if the fort came under attack.

Above:
The staff of CPIC in Chonqing welcoming me to their offices.

2nd May 2006

Road to Chongqing was very easy, 294 Km, dual carriageway the whole way, found the Hotel Chongqing Guest House which is old and relatively comfortable. Good to get to Chongqing as have a rest day and get the laundry done.

At 2.00pm Trupin Tang of CPIC came around and took my oxygen gas cylinders to be filled and then we drove up to CPIC's offices and as we arrived at the main gate there were all the staff lined up in a line and clapping as I entered the forecourt, rather moving. Then it was shaking hands all round and a Group photograph on the steps with the car in the foreground. After this we went up to the meeting room where I had to describe the journey so far and forthcoming sections. The Chairman, who I had not met before, apparently is very interested in travelling and wanted to join me and was so supportive of the journey.

Then I met a reporter of the local daily, the article was to appear the next day (which it did)

Met my new guide Joe, who comes from Chongqing and is 36.

That evening Mr. Tang invited me to an excellent dinner at a restaurant that I had been to on my first visit from Dubai.

CPIC is another fibreglass manufacturer, also of a very high standard.

3rd May 2006

CPIC had rented the Central Hall Square in order to make a presentation to me. The staff and their families of CPIC had been invited, plus the general public, to witness the Ceremony. It started off by Chinese Lady Drummers dressed in red, beating drums, which is the traditional way of sending someone off on a journey or a great occasion. Then there were the speeches by Mr. Wu, the Chairman and Mr. Tang, the General Manager, followed by myself. CPIC presented me with a cheque for RMB 100,000.00 (US$ 12,500.00) and was told that other Chongqing companies had also donated money, one Company RMB 30,000 etc., and individuals in the square donated on the spot up to US$ 2,000.00 and signed their names on a roll of red silk that I still have. The day raised approximately US$ 25,000.00. This money also went to Orbis China.

The Press and the Chongqing TV were all present. CPIC said that they would send a copy of the film to me in the UK.

Later on, I visited the highest point in Chongqing and from the top of a Pagoda took photographs on a 360 degree view of Chongqing, which was interesting. I then visited the People's Museum, which showed the history of Chongqing, well presented and displayed.

In the evening I went out to dinner with Joe, the guide, to a restaurant on the Yangtse, which was good and then went to a bar owned by a friend of his on the bank of the Yangtse.

Left:
A view looking down on to the Yangtse that will change when the river fills to the top of the grass bank on the completion of the Three Gorges Dam.

庆出发仪式
CPIC
重庆国际复合材料有限公司 向"光明行动"捐赠
Donation to Orbis in Aid of "18000KM to Save Sight" by CPIC
人民币壹拾万元整
A sum of RMB100,000 only
2006年5月3日
May 3rd 2006

捐赠处

Above:
The Dazu Grotto, which is over 800 years old.

Opposite page top:
Being presented with a cheque by the Chairman and Managing Director of CPIC in Chongqing.

Opposite page bottom:
Members of Chongqing donating a total of $1,500.00 for Orbis in the Chongqing Square.

4th May 2006

Drove to Chengdu along a very good road and arrived at 4.00pm after 335 km but en-route diverted off the main road to the Dazu Grotto. The Grotto is an enormous cliff carving of various scenes of the Buddhist faith, carved 800 years ago and which avoided destruction by the Red Guards during the Cultural Revolution. The carvings are the scenes of the Buddhist faith and what one should and should not do in respecting ones parents and elders.

Stayed at the Tibet Hotel which was comfortable, went out to inner with my new guide Lily, Chen Chun, had an excellent dinner.

5th May 2006.

Stayed in Chengdu and in the morning went to the Panda Sanctuary which is stunning, the animals look really well and well

cared for. All the keepers wear throw away overalls and gloves to try and ensure the human smell does not rub off on the animals as one day they want to send the strongest back in to the forests, to date only ne has successfully been restored.

Each pen is large, has climbing frames, trees and areas to roam in as well as water pools as Pandas need to drink a lot in order to digest the food. The bamboo is cut daily and trucked in from a 2 hour drive distance, it is washed and fed to the Pandas four times a day. When eating they lie back and pick stalks of bamboo, first peeling the outer hard skin off in their teeth and then chewing the inner stem. Only about 20 % of the bamboo gets converted in to energy the rest passes through their body. They chew on average for 16 hours a day.

In Chengdu they have bred 181 babies to date of whom some 45% have survived, for the first 18 months of life they stay with their mother and then go off on their own, they are a solitary animal. I bought a DVD of the sanctuary.

Above:
The seated Buddha at the Dazu Grotto.

Opposite page top:
Three baby Pandas playing at the Panda sanctuary in Chengdu.

Opposite page bottom:
Three happy pandas quietly eating bamboo at Chengdu Panda sanctuary.

Opposite page:
The largest Buddha, carved out of sandstone, at Leshan, standing at 71 metres high.

In the afternoon I went to the Central Park, where the elderly were singing Karaoke in a tea hous. There must have been 250 people watching and applauding.

In the evening after dinner I went to a concert of culture, which was brilliant. The programme consisted of a traditional Sechuan Band with Operatic excerpts being played, followed by a fantastic hand shadow display of birds flying and pecking, a swan, a dog chasing a rabbit, catching it and swallowing it (you see the rabbit going down the throat by the movement of the hand), a horse trotting and galloping. Then there was a type of lyre, a Chinese violin called the Erhu. The man playing it just created the most beautiful flowing melodic tunes from the instrument.

6th May 2006

Met up with my new guide Tsering, a young Tibetan, who reminds me very much of the Gurkhas to look at. This is the first time that he has been to China, so he was quite excited. We drove off to Leshan with Lily, thus I had two guides. Leshan is famous for the Great Buddha that was carved out of Red Sand Stone some 1200 years ago. The carving of the 71 meter high statue was supervised by a monk, as the spot where it stands is at the confluence of three rivers that make up the Mein Jiang, which ultimately flows in to the Yangtse in Chongqing. Many fishermen have been drowned here and so the statue was built to appease the devil.

Luckily the main statue was not damaged or defaced by the Red Guards, but smaller figures running down the side of the walkways, for the tourists, were decapitated.

7th May 2006

Drove from Leshan to Kangding through the mountains, 360 km. It was a beautiful drive with the road was good all the way and not too much traffic. We saw some snow capped mountain tops. for the first time. The journey was really good, the Oil Seed Rape was being harvested, cut by hand and stacked. The highest point was 2,100 meters, but the mountain through which a tunnel had been cut was 4,100 meters high.

When we arrived in Kangding we eventually found a hotel which was basic, but perfectly pleasant. There was no internet available. We walked about 1½ km to a Tibetan Namo Monastry, which was very interesting. In the evening I went to a Tibetan restaurant and I am afraid to say that I do not like the Tibetan Butter Tea, it is oily and rich - I am sorry to say that I could only take a couple of sips.

Left:
The melting snow races down the river through Kangding.

Above:
The Namo Monastery in Kangding.

8th May 2006

We drove from Kangding to Litang, a distance of 291 km, and went over three passes all over 4,000 meters. The first was 4,167m, the second 4,659 metres and the third 4,718 meters above sea level. The road was, in places, was very bad and most was unmade stoney mud track. The scenery was magical and you could see thousands of Yak across the hillsides. The snow line seemed to be at 4,000 meters and the leaves had only recently come out. The tree line was at about 3,600 meters. From the photographs you can see the change in scenery.

Litang is a small town where we had a good dinner in a pleasant hotel, the Pilgrima Hotel. It boasted with squat loos. The staff were very nice and chatty to the guide.

Left
A yurt on the road from Kangding to Litang.

Left:
A Buddhist Stuppa on a high pass on the road to Litang.

Left:
A pass at 4,718 metres above sea level on the road to Litang.

9th May 2006

I decided to set off early leaving the hotel at 7.45am in order to be ahead of the traffic and if possible to leap-frog Batang and go straight to Markam in Tibet. To begin with the road was good and for the first 25 kilometers we did not see another vehicle going in our direction. We had one pass to cross at 4,689 meters. After the pass and having dropped about 1,000 meters, we picked up the most diabolical bit of road that went on for 40 kilometers. The road was badly broken up and in places they were constructing a new road, so there were diversions. These were terrible with deep puddles, ruts and where they had laid new culverts there were small ramps up and over. I think a small car would have difficulty crossing without catching the underside.In a few places you could not go more then 5kph and even then bottomed out, gently, once or twice. After Batang there was a further 15 kilometers of bad road, but then, when we came to the Tibet border the route improved, albeit unmade-up road. The scenery was wonderful with deep gorges. Quite a lot of barley and wheat was being grown in the river basins and occasionally we came across isolated houses and hamlets.

On approaching Markam, the scenery changed to bare hills. On one side the hills had very short grass, as first thing in the morning there was still a frost. On the northerly side the hills were red stone with the odd tree. The farms were looking good.

We stayed at the Kargcur Hotel, which was named after a lake. The hotel is Tibetan run and obviously popular. It has all the facilities, but the electricity only came on at 6.00pm. I had a good dinner of rice and yak meat, which was tender and tasty.

After dinner I washed the car, as it was filthy. It was caked in mud from the drive.

Overleaf top:
A yak being used to plough a field on the road to Markham.

Overleaf bottom:
The Volvo XC90 is caked with mud.

亚泉高速
川V.04116
04116

10th May 2006

My original plan was to drive from Markam to Basu, some 380 km. Provided the road was not too rough we would endeavour to go on to Bome, a further 212 km, as then we could get to Nyinchi and be back online, hopefully, able to upload the photographs for the website.

To begin with, the road was a rough road, but with a generally good surface. We had two passes to cross, the highest being 4,618 meters. The greatest problem with these roads is that they are all dry and therefore dusty. You can see from a long way off whether a vehicle coming towards or going away. However, the dust is like powder and permeates the AC.

Saw two pheasant, a fox, a buzzard and a lot of small song birds, as well as crows and magpies. The farms, again, were looking good. Hundreds/thousands of Yak, many horses and goats, sheep and donkeys and two chipmunks.

Coming off the high pass it took an hour and a half to get out of the mountain range as the road was poor, but not disastrous. One photograph shows the forthcoming road zig-zagging away.

After Basu the road improved to tarmac, which pushed us on nicely. But after Basu some 40 km later we again came onto a rough road and you could see many areas where stone falls had occurred and half blocked the road. Near to Bome we came across a lot of wild rhododendrons that were in full flower.

I was pleased to get to Bome at 6.30pm, as we had been going for 10 hours, but great news was that it now meant that we were back on our timetable and so we would be able to have the two days as planned in Nyinchi and be able to have an extra day in Lhasa and Shigatse.

Previous page top: Following a bus along the main road en-route to Batang.

Previous page bottom: A high pass on the road to Batang.

Right:
Still following the bus on the washed-out road to Batang.

Right:
The road to Bome with a sheer drop from the unbarriered road.

Above:
A man with a monk (just out of the picture to the right), drinking water on the washed out highway on the road from Bome to Nyinchi.

Opposite page:
Looking back along the road with the fields way below.

11th May 2006

We drove the 230 km from Bome to Nyinchi. We first had breakfast in a normal roadside café and there was a little girl all dressed for school, with satchel on her back, having breakfast, but glued to the television. The food was hardly going into her mouth, she was so engrossed with the programme.

The road was very bad once we got off the tarmac and it was drizzling, which had started to make the powder dust slippery. The road was desperately narrow and in no way could two vehicles pass. I would have hated to reverse any distance as traction was not good. In one place I went up a steep slope and when I got to the top could not see where the road went on the other side - quite scarry! This section was definitely only for one vehicle. Shortly afterwards we crossed a stream running about 12 inches deep across the road.

There were three sections of rough road/dirt track on this road and the tarmac, where it existed, was excellent. It rained steadily and at the top of the pass before dropping down to Nyinchi it was even

Above:
A bridge that I had to cross, I realised it was safe as a lorry was about to cross but had to go on to a weigh-bridge first.

sleeting. Sadly, due to cloud cover, we were not able to see the main mountain, which is 7,800 meters high.

This whole stretch was very different from all the others as we passed through forests and the colours were lovely, as the leaves had only recently opened. A lot of the rhododendrons were in full bloom. In this area there were a lot of cows and pigs with a few yak. I even saw a weasel or stoat!

Left:
A little school girl having breakfast, but who did not take her eyes off the television.

12th May 2006

Today was a rest day in Nyinchi. Went to see the Lamaling Monastery about 30 km from Nyinchi. The Monastery was first built in about AD 800 by a Nepalese Lama, but was burned down and rebuilt at a lower location some 100+ years ago following an earthquake. It was again destroyed during the Cultural Revolution in 1966 and rebuilt in 1987.

There were some Peone trees with yellow and Pink flowers, which were very attractive, together with a ram and three Blue Sheep. The ram was smelling peoples shoes and then walked in to the Monastery, before being chased off.

Tsering bought a string of Prayer Flags which he took around the Monastery to be blessed and then wrote our names on each flag to give us good luck and long life.

We next went to the World High Cyprus Park which has about 50 – 60 *Cyprus Giganta*, one of which is dated as being 2,600 years old. This one is 50 meters tall and has a girth of 5.1 meters. I saw a number of grey squirrels on the tree and heard a cuckoo fairly close by. As we left the Park an attractive Tibetan girl tried to sell us Herbs.

The day was showery.

Below: Lamaling Monastery in Nyinchi.

Left:
A 2,600 year old Cyprus Giganta in the reserve at Nyinchi. Its girth is 5.1 meters and the tree is 50 meters high.

Left:
A Blue Sheep at the entrance to the Lamaling Monastery.

13th May 2006

Drove the 417 km from Nyinchi to Lhasa. It rained the whole way and the further up the hills we went it sleeted and snowed. The scenery was very different to that from Bome to Nyinchi. Here it varied from green and forestry to mountainous. Passing over the only pass at 5,000 meters, the road was reduced to one lane due to snow at the top of the pass. There were prayer flags everywhere! On the run down to Lhasa we passed along the left side of a wide valley that was being heavily farmed with barley and wheat, whilst closer to Lhasa there were a few miles of plastic tunnel farming.

The initial view of the Potala Palace was exactly as one had imagined. It appeared suddenly as we rounded a corner. Unfortunately we could not stop there to take a photograph. It looked like a building that basically appeared to be on its own, but in reality is not. We then drove int the city and passed directly in front of the Palace, which was fabulous. Tsering took a photograph just to show we had arrived, but tomorrow we will take more, as we will be visiting the Potala Palace at midday.

We stayed at the Lhasa Hotel that used to be a Holiday Inn, but which has since been returned to the Government management. This showed in the levels of service. The rooms do not have Internet, but the Business Centre has a fast connection, so am able to use that.

In the evening went to a good restaurant and had a Nepali Curry of Yak meat which was good. Unfortunately and completely my fault I damaged the right front wing when parking to go to the restaurant and broke part of the head light glass. I have hopefully done a repair that will hold.

14th May 2006

First we went to the Summer Palace, which has two main Palaces: the first that was built by the 7th Dalai Lama and the last in 1954-56 by the present Dalai Lama within a Garden of 360,000 square meters. The distance from the Potala Palace is only 3 miles but is set in pleasant gardens that have many varieties of trees.

The Summer Palace built by the current Dalai Lama has many

small, but sparsely furnished rooms. The Dalai Lama's chairs/thrones are very wide. I was presented with a white scarf and Buddhist medallion for the car and to bring good luck. Both are still in my car.

At midday we went to the Potala Palace, which consists of two Palaces: the White Palace, which was built in 1645 and became the Government seat of office advising the Dalai Lama, and the Red Palace, which was built in 1690 to hold the Stupa Tomb of the 5th Dalai Lama. In 1934 there was a further high building built to house the Golden Stupa Tomb of the 13th Dalai Lama.

In the evening walked around the Barkhor, a busy shopping area that sells anything from Yak Butter to Incense, nicknacks, fake jewelry and some better shops that have some genuine antiques.

Above
The last rather cold pass before dropping down to Lhasa from Nyinchi.

Right:
The Potala Palace.

Right:
The Dalai Lama's Summer Palace.

Left:
The entrance to the Potala Palace. Notice the walls are built leaning inwards to strengthen the building in case of earthquakes.

Left:
The Potala Palace.

Above: The Summer Palace in Lhasa.

15th May 2006

In the morning went around the Jokhang Temple by the Barkhor Square. The Holy days every month are the 1st, 8th, 15th and 30th. As a result, there were hundreds of Tibetans visiting the Temple and praying some making abeyances and others putting Yak butter on to the Candle holders - the smell in certain areas was really rather noxious. There were dozens of small crypts where candles were burning in Yak butter and statues of the different Dalai Lamas, or of the 33rd King who brought Buddhism to Tibet from India and Nepal.

Unfortunately only the emergency lights were on and so the candle light was the only sort of lighting available. It was really not enough to see the statues properly.

In the afternoon wandered around the streets of Lhasa.

16th May 2006.

I went to the Drepung Monastery, the first major Monastery in

Tibet. Here you were able to see most of the buildings. The entrance ticket is a CD of the Monastery as inside you cannot take photographs.

The Monastery originally built in 1416 and was enlarged in the 16th century. It used to be the home of 10,000 Monks, but now only has 1,000. The Assembly Hall is the largest in Tibet and has 108 pillars. Breakfast and dinner is eaten in the Assembly Hall daily and it was able to seat the 10,000 monks, before the Red Cultural Revolution.

In the afternoon we went on to the Sera Monastery, which is the second largest in Lhasa and was built in 1419. It was open to the public and was interesting to see in the courtyard a few hundred monks testing each other on the scriptures. The questioner stands up and if the answer is correct he will bring his right hand down on the left in a sweeping clap. If the answer is wrong then he will bring the back of his right hand down and explain why the answer was wrong.

In the evening we went to the Shangri-la restaurant for a buffet dinner and there we watched traditional dancing and singing, which was very colourful .

Above:
Looking down from the Barkhor Monastery with the Potala Palace in the distance.

Right:
Looking down to the Lhasa valley from the Drepung Monastry.

Right:
Monks being taught and tested on the scriptures.

Above:
The Drepung Monastry.

17th May 2006

We drove from Lhasa south to Shigatse, 68 km south of Lhasa. Turning off the main road, we drove 32 km up a series of hills until we came to the summit at 4,990 meters that overlooked a large lake, Yamdrok-tso. The climb was about 1,300 meters on an excellent road. The views were stunning and again we were blessed with bright blue sky. The snow covered mountains in the far distance were clearly reflected in the lake. At the top there were 20+ local Tibetans with their Yaks, a baby blue sheep and dogs wanting their photographs taken for a few RMB.

The scenery on the way to Shigatse went through 4 phases. Firstly, the Lhasa river running through a wide valley with farmland, then through a long ravine narrow, but excellent road with a river on the left and very little greenery to be seen. Thirdly, out of the ravine just over half way to Shigatse there were sand dunes and sand blown up the mountain sides. Finally coming on to the Shigatse plain it was very wide and heavily cultivated with barley and in areas watermelons being grown under plastic.

In many areas along the route we saw many new villages that have been built for the locals. The buildings are of stone with carved eaves and window frames so very colourful. These houses do not have internal loos, but communal ones, which I suppose is the only draw back. Again all the animals were well cared for.

We stayed at the Shigatse Hotel, which is of a higher standard compared to the Lhasa Hotel and the staff appeared to be better trained. I had lunch in a little café, which was excellent - rice, bacon and vegetables, leaks and Yak meat with potatoes and green tea.

In the afternoon went to the Zhashenlunbu Temple Monastery that was built in 1447. The Monastery holds the Tomb of the fifth Panchen Lama and was rebuilt by the 10th Panchen Lama in 1989 and the Government gave RMB 64m towards the cost. It also holds the second largest Assembly Hall, which once held over 3,500 Monks, but now has only about 1,000 left. The Monastery was less vandalised than most during the Cultural Revolution.

Right:
Zhashenlumbu Temple Monastry, built in 1447 for the Yellow Hat monks.

Opposite page: top
The beautiful lake Yamsok-tso 100 km south of Lhasa.

18th May 2006

Drove down to Gyantse which is only 90 km from Shigatse. The road was good and flat, running along the river and wide valley, which is heavily farmed. There were very few trees of any age, other than the willows that run along the roadside. There are also many small tractors, that we did not see in China, carrying goods, but there was ploughing in the fields being done by oxen, yak and horses. You could see all three working in one field. The valley is up to 3 miles wide in places. We passed through many new villages, which without doubt has helped those Tibetans that were poor.

Next we went to the Pala Manor which is about 5 km from Gyantse, the Pala family were one of the main Tibetan families, alongside that of the Dalai Lama's, but going around the Pala Manor it became clear how badly, right up to 1959, the people who worked for the major families were treated. The accommodation that was given to the peasants was terrible and they were paid a pittance according to the job they did. After 1959 and Independence, the takeover of Tibet by China, the peasants were given land and are now earning good money from their small holdings, as well as being given housing.

The first place we visited was the Gyantse Baiju Temple. The temple was built in 1418 and the Stupa was built in the Nepalese style in 1427. The Baiju Stupa was not over impressive, but interesting. The Stupa has 108 small temples with over 100,000 images. The view from the top of the Stupa was interesting and looked out over the wide plain and towards the Gyantse Castle (Fort).

The Gyantse Fort was approached by driving through the back streets of Gyantse and there we saw cattle and horses tethered outside the houses. With difficulty, I meandered the car through the animals and drove half way up the hill to the fort. The fort was originally built in AD 967 and was extended in 1390. It stands on top of a hill that must be 200 meters plus higher than the town below and so was difficult to attack. Captain Younghusband of the British Army took a force of more than 500 soldiers in 1889 to capture the fort that resulted in a massacre of more than 500 Tibetans, many of whom committed suicide by jumping off the walls of the fort. Nearly at the top of the

Opposite page bottom:
Black and White Yak with their owners at Yamsok-tso.

Left:
Gyantse Fort with an old wooden cannon used against the British.

Left:
Two British cannons at Gyantse Fort that were rather more superior to the Tibetan cannon.

hill leading up to the Fort there are two British heavy cannon as well as two wooden barrelled Tibetan cannon. Down in the town there is a new museum that is an anti-British memorial that remembers the heroes of the resistance.

We lunched at a Tibetan restaurant in Gyantse which was good. After the visit to the Pala Manor, we drove back to Shigatse.

Above:
Gyantse Baiju Temple.

19th May 2006

Drove from Shigatse to Lhasa, a distance of 270 km.

Upon arrival, I went to CITS office to try and sort out repayment of money from the Insurance Company.

I noticed that virtually all the snow on the surrounding mountain tops had melted, which loses some of the majestic scenery

I picked up a copy of an article that was written in the Lhasa Press and as published on the 18th May. I had to say goodbye to Tsering, who had been a wonderful, always smiling and cheerful guide, I genuinely believe that he thoroughly enjoyed our trip, as it was so different to what he normally experienced.

20th May 2006

When I left Lhasa with my new Guide, a young Chinese man aged 26, Mathew, it was raining quite heavily. The route to NaQu, which is at 4,400 meters ran along-side the brand new railway line

Above:
The road going to Shigatse, south of Lhasa.

from Xining to Lhasa. As we started to climb up in to the hills the rain turned to snow and was settling on the ground. Combined with a strong wind, the dry snow was being blown off the hills.

Eventually, we climbed up out of the hills and on to the Tibetan Plateau. Although the weather was not ideal, the scenery was all that I had imagined - enormous flat grassland that stretched nearly as far as the eye could see, until the next range of hills came in to view. There were thousands of yak grazing and nearer to the small hamlets, that popped up from time to time, you then saw horses and sheep and goats. Out on the plains there were the Nomads' black tents that are made from yak skins

At one point we saw a diesel train engine and four flat trucks testing out the new railway line. I was told that the carriages will be pressurised so as to help the travellers avoid altitude sickness. Every 100 meters or so culverts have been built so that the Yak etc. can move under the track and cross to new pastures. The line is built up about 5 meters above the grassland level so the construction has been a massive

Right:
A pass going up on to the Tibetan Plateau north of Lhasa on the road to NaQu.

task of moving earth, stone, building bridges, tunnels and so on. The line will be officially opened on the 1st July 2006, just over a month from today. We passed three enormous convoys of Army lorries, each consisting of about 100 vehicles. The drivers were well disciplined as they left a lot of room for other traffic to overtake and tuck in safely.

We arrived in NaQu, which is a town of about 30,000 people. It was really quite dirty and untidy. My hotel for the night, the NaQu Hotel is being modernised and decorated throughout. The room was clean and well furnished, but as anticipated no Internet. I have no doubt that it will arrive within the next year, as more travellers stop off from the railway. The temperature was hovering around 5°C, whilst it was snowing the temperature dropped to 1°C.

After lunch we walked around the town which consisted of a lot of small shops, including shoe makers and seamstresses with old Singer-style machines, lots of motor and building merchants, as there is a lot of building construction going on in the whole area.

In the evening went to a Tibetan Restaurant which was amusing. We had a good dinner and had my picture taken with two Tibetans, who were very nice and interested in the strange foreigner. As we left I had to go to the kitchen which was amazingly clean and had picture taken with the cook and two waitresses.

Opposite page top: Rolling grassland for as far as the eye can see with yak grazing and a small hamlet.

21st May 2006

We were meant to have stopped in a small town just over the Tanggula Pass, but it transpired there was no hotel, which the guide had an inkling was likely to be the case. So we left NaQu at 7.00am and drove through to Golmud.

The day was glorious sunshine, but cold from 7.00am to 12 noon the temperature hovered at 0°C to -5°C. The scenery is terribly difficult to describe, as you have miles upon miles of open grasslands, which are still all brown or yellow semi dead grass, with areas that are swamp with tussocks of grass and small up to large lakes dotting the land. The lakes reflect the blue sky and so the colour is wonderful. In the background you can see the snow capped peaks that encircle the pastureland. Below the snowline you see the nomad's tents and yak, horses and sheep.

We went over two high peaks 5,170 and 5,231 meters high. The road in places was excellent, but in others was subsiding. Without warning you would hit a hollow that did not clearly show up. We passed three convoys of Army lorries going in to Tibet; each convoy was 25 vehicles strong.

The town where we were meant to have stopped for the night was a one street place full of vehicle repair shops and no hotel to be seen. After lunch we went to the spot which is said to be the source of the Yangtse river and marked by a plaque.

Along the whole route the new railway ran. The train journey should be a really scenic and fascinating one once it becomes operational from 1st July 2006 - 6 weeks time.

After we crossed the final pass, we came to gravel flatlands with a certain amount of sand. Once more, in the sunlight, the colours were wonderful.

Once we arrived in Golmud we were confronted with a very organized and clean town of 300,000 population. There were broad streets lined with trees. Our overnight rest was at the Golmud Hotel, which has 3 stars.

Opposite page bottom: A train testing the new railway line being built from Xining to Lhasa.

Above:
The highest pass at 5,231 meters above sea level and broken up road. The temperature was -5°C.

Opposite page top:
The rolling plains up on the Tibetan plateau, sea shells can be found on the ground.

Opposite page bottom:
The gravel road and lying snow on the Tibetan Plateau.

22nd May 2006

A quiet day in and around Golmud. We first went to the Forest reserve, which was some 60km from Golmud past the airport. 50km was dirt road with the last km a sand track. When we eventually arrived, there was only brushwood that was just beginning to sprout, a stone plaque and two nomad's summer tents that acted as a hotel, should anyone actually want to stay. Close by there was a river that flowed and overspilled in to wetlands into which I saw a pair of duck fly. The whole area was infested with mosquitoes.

From the main road, the dirt road ran through pebble flatland until we came to a farm that had water diverted from a river and where there were mature trees and small fields of barley. As we got to the area of the forest, we came to the sand dunes with brush wood.

After lunch back in Golmud, we walked around the market area and saw good fresh fruit, vegetables, live fish and meat being fly-whisked. The quality generally looked good.

Above:
The road that was meant to lead to a forest that no longer existed.

23rd May 2006

Drove to Dunhuang, 543 km in distance. Probably a very interesting sight, except today the weather was overcast with a mist. The first 40 km was tarmac and then the next 140 km was a stone / shale road. On the whole not bad as the Chinese were rebuilding the main road. 85 km out from Golmud we passed about 20 km of soda salt flats. This area is the largest soda salt processing region in China. The scenery was difficult to see because of the weather.

The last 40 km to Dunhuang was through initially gravel and then some impressive sand dunes.

The Hotel Grand Sun Hotel is good.

24th May 2006

In the morning visited the Mogao Grottoes, 25 km from Dunhuang. The oasis of Dunhuang stretches about 70 km and is full of wheat, rice, vegetables and cotton fields. About 18 km from Dunhuang we turned right down a straight road that led to the famous Mogao Caves, which have been carved in to sandstone. The caves were lost for centuries and were only rediscovered in the early 1900s.

The earliest cave was constructed in AD 366. In total there are 735 caves, of which 490 have either statues of Buddha and or Murals. Each cave used to have an outer hall, corridor, no more than 15 feet long, then the main chamber that would have a statue of Buddha and murals on all the walls and ceilings. Most were constructed in the 6th century AD with a certain amount of alteration to some in the 11th century.

There was an inner chamber in one cave that was used for the burial of a renowned monk, This was sealed up and remained unnoticed until 1900. In the cave over 50,000 manuscripts and paintings were

Below:
Dromedary camels on the road from Golmud to Dunhuang.

found, which had been hidden from potential marauders. Many of these were taken to the British Museum and Guilmet Museum, in Paris, which at the time may have been correct, as many of the ones that remained were distributed around nobles in China rather than going to the Museum in Beijing.

I bought a DVD of the Mogoa Grottoes.

In the afternoon we went to The Mingsha Mountains and Crescent Spring about 5 km south of Dunhuang. It was a lovely afternoon, hot at 33°C and so I decided to walk, rather than take a camel or open bus to the Mountain and Crescent Spring, a distance across the sand. We were forced to buy a bottle of water, which was sensible. There were a good two hundred Dromedary Camels ready to take the tourists. Firstly, I walked to a little farming village where they were growing onions, cotton and two other crops. The irrigation is fed by natural sweet water springs that flows in to a small lake. The lake was part surrounded by reeds and you could hear bullfrogs croaking. From there I went over a little sand dune and came to see the most magical sight - that of the Crescent Spring, which looks like a new moon. Rising above it

Below:
Camels taking tourists to the Crescent Springs and Buddhist temple outside Dunhuang.

was a wooden Pagoda built around the 11th century. The sand dunes completely encircle the oasis and for some unknown reason the sand has never drifted or touched the Spring. The Dunes are 300 meters high.

From the Pagoda we walked up steps to the top of the 300 meter sand dune. How I hate steps! After a few breathers, the view from the top was well worth the effort, because it really outlined the small area of natural water, green grass and the Pagoda surrounded by the dunes. The cover of this book shows this fabulous scene.

Nearly half way down, we walked about 100 meters off to the left and there hired a sand board and went the rest of the way down on a sand board, I am glad to say that other than one steering correction I went hell for leather to the bottom. Sher my guide fell off half way down so I was well satisfied. A great afternoon.

Below right:
The five storey entrance to the Mogoa Buddhist tombs.

Below left:
Wooden Pagoda built around AD 1200 at Crescent Spring outside Dunhuang, a most beautiful spot totally surrounded by sand dunes 1000 feet high.

JUST
BRING
IT!

Opposite page top:
The wooden temple in the paradise of the sweet water crescent spring amazingly not swallowed up by the dunes.

Opposite page bottom:
Sher looking down on to the Crescent Spring.

25th May 2006

Today, we drove out from Dunhuang into the Gobi Desert for about 180 km. Firstly, we stopped some 40km from Dunhuang at the Yumen Pass (Gate). This gate was an important crossing point for all travellers that wanted to cross the Gobi Desert. They had to stop at the pass to give a final feed and watering to their camels, if they were about to cross the desert, because the next nearest watering hole was 20 days by camel, averaging 20-25 km a day. All travellers had to pay their dues. On the north side of the Gate there is a large lake with grassland so the camels could forage.

From there we went a further 60 km to one of the few remaining sections of the Han Wall, this piece being the furthest west. In olden times the Han Wall joined with the Great Wall of China and the total

Below:
Dunhuang Fruit Market.

distance covered was in excess of 5000km. The wall is made of mud blocks piled on top of each other. Sadly, most seems either to have eroded or been taken away.

Then after a further 80 km we came to the Geological Park of the World, which was originally a large lake in the Gobi, but many thousands of years ago it dried up, leaving mounds of sandstone that over time has been eroded by the wind, sandstorms and rain. Some of the rocks have taken on fascinating shapes such as a tortoise, peacock on top of a rock, a slight replica of the Sphinx and many many other shapes. Every year the scenery changes as erosion continues. One pillar that is quite slight is expected to collapse over the next two years. This was yet another day that I thoroughly enjoyed, as the world has so many fascinating natural and spectacular sites to see.

Below:
The Gobi Desert and a peacock created by erosion of wind, rain and water.

26th May 2006

Today, we drove to Hami, but as there was nothing to see there we carried on to Turpan, 835km away. The scenery throughout the journey was a vast open gravel stone desert, in many places, with no vegetation what so ever, until you come upon an oasis, which is where Hami is situated. The road was good the whole way, which made a real change.

After Hami, we came to a village some 46 km from Turpan, called Tuik. Tuik was originally populated by seven followers of the Prophet Mohamed, who translated the Koran in to the Uyger language and persuaded the then Buddhists to change faith. In Tuik there are

Below:
A view from Tuik to the Buddhist tombs.

caves that originally had statues of Buddha and murals, but these were defaced and the locals were forbidden to worship Buddha.

The village, as is today, remains as it must have been 300 years ago - small mud houses with grapes and mulberry trees all around. The village is nestled into the mountains and a great effort has been made to make the caves accessible to tourists, by building walkways and steps.

From Tuik, we drove down the valley some 250 feet below sea level. On the east side there were oil derricks and pumping donkeys. Oil was first extracted here 15 years ago.

We are staying at the Grand Turban Hotel. We went out to dinner in the open square and had very good lamb followed by noodles, vegetable soup which was also good.

Below:
Buddhist tombs that had wonderful murals that have been destroyed.

Above:
Tuik village that has not changed for 300 years, many centenarians live there.

27th May 2006

Today first drove to the Ancient City of Gaochang about 37 km from Turpan the first construction was in the 1st Century BC, it was built by the Western Han Dynasty's Imperial garrison troops, the second phase of building took place between the 4-7th Century AD, during this period the Tang Dynasty set up the Western Prefecture and five counties were ruled from Gaochang. In the 9th – 13th century Gaochang became the capital of the Huihu Gaochang Kingdom until it was destroyed during the tenure of Ghengis Khan's son.

The City was built of mud brick with little comfort but the mud kept the air cool in the house compared to the scorching sun that can reach 48C. Each phase of the development had its own perimeter wall the outer wall stretches 5 km. A river from the Bezelik Caves and the flaming Mountains fed the City with fresh water. The City in its heyday had a population of 30,000. One corner of the City was destroyed during the Cultural Revolution when local peasants demolished buildings and grew crops in the mud that was broken down by destroying the

houses until they were thrown off the land in 1981 when the City was recognized as a site of historical value.

Above:
The Bezelik Caves that had wonderful frescoes.

Then visited the Ancient Astana Tombs that are only about 3 km from Gaochang and was used as the Muslim Burial grounds. The bodies were mummified and kept particularly well as the air is so dry. We saw two bodies one of a woman in her 60s and one of a younger man. Two of the tombs had very interesting murals with 12 natural materials one telling the story of life from the Jade man that represented the purity of a new born baby, to the stone man that had to experience things in life, to the wood man who needed to learn through to the old man who should stay at home and teach his life's experience to his family. The other paintings were painted for a General who had moved from Eastern China and he got a local painter to paint six pictures of different birds and plants that grew in his original eastern homeland. The colours are very good. There have been over 500 mummies excavated as well as many thousands of carvings, fabrics and manuscripts discovered.

We then went to the Bezelik Thousand Buddha Caves about 8 km from Astana, which are up in the Flaming Mountains. The Flaming Mountains are named due to the red colour, which in the right light looks as though they are on fire. The caves were cut in to the sand stone starting in AD 499 until AD 640, The statues have all gone as have most of the murals either by a German adventurer Le Coq who visited the area in the early 1900s. He paid a small amount of money and removed many Buddhist statues, transferring them to Berlin by Camel, but many were destroyed in transit. The local Muslims defaced the rest during the 16th Century, when they tried to drive all the Buddhists away from the area. The caves are above the river that fed the Gaochang Ancient City and today there are a few small farms growing vines. It is a very tranquil area thanks to the river, mountains and few trees giving some shade to the vineyards. I even heard a cuckoo was calling in the background.

From there we drove 30 km down a track, which was meant to have been a road to the lake in the basin of the Depression, the second lowest point on earth at 154 meters below sea level. The journey was a bit tedious, as initially there was just gravel. We ran into a bit of farming activity and then nothing, other than brown earth, which had been cleaned of the salt crystals and dumped back on to the land. We passed though deserted villages, which had been once on the lake's shore, but

Below:
Having tea with a a102 year old man and his grand daughter in Turpan.

over time the waters dropped, the size of the lake decreased and the people moved. Some of the salt crystals were very large.

In the evening we went to the Valley of Grapes, to the north of Turpan, which was interesting. In the greater Turpan area, 660 million tons of grapes are grown annually apparently, some for the making of wine, others for dried fruit and fresh grapes. All together there are over 700 different varieties of vines in the area. We drove through small villages with all the houses festooned in vine arbours, which were most attractive. We went to the Grape Valley Centre where many farmers were selling their dried fruit, the new crop not as yet being ready. I had a raisin tasting session, which was most interesting and bought ½ kilo of two different varieties. I tasted a few wines that were reasonable and in the style of the Southern French wines, so bought two bottles to take home.

We went to two buildings; one that was built in the style of the local Turpan people and the other in the Kashgar style, which was much more ornate. The complete buildings and trellis were built by my guide's father who is a Master Craftsman from Kashgar and who has built many buildings in the Kashgar style for the Government throughout China.

I had my photograph taken with a 102 year old Uygur and his great niece an 18 year old.

Dinner, again, in the People's Square which was excellent.

Below:
Sher paying for our supper of spit roast lamb in the Turpan open market.

Above:
The ancient city of Jiaohe, close to Turpan.

28th May 2006

We first went to the Ancient City of Jiaohe about 13 km north of Turpan. Jiaohe is like an island surrounded by two small rivers that join at the Southern end and is 30 meters above the river bed with sheer sand stone Cliff faces. The City was first built in the 2nd century BC and then expanded, like Gaochang, in the 7th century AD. It had a maximum population of 7,000. The City was destroyed, again like Gaochang, by Tamerlane in the 13th Century, because the locals would not convert from Buddhism to Islam.

The City has three Buddhist Temples, a large Stupa and 100 smaller ones that no longer exist. The City is in a better state of repair than Gaochang. The city is very well laid out for the tourist.

From Jiaohe we went to the Museum of the Karez water irrigation system, which was most interesting. The Tianshan Mountains have snow all the year round and the melt water seeps in to the rock and accumulates. The Turpan district is very arid and has no rain at all other than about three times a year when a few millimetres might fall. Despite this, the ground happens to be very fertile. About two thousand years ago a King instructed some peasants to dig a channel from the Tianshan Mountains to the Turpan area. In all, there are 163,068 Karez Wells that vary in depth from 98 meters to 20 meters. The wells were joined every 5 - 10 meters by tunnels hewn out by hand. The water is very sweet and flows at a constant rate all the year round. The total length of all the tunnels is some 5,000km. Every year the tunnels are cleaned out, in case there have been any rock falls or silt has collected. Originally the locals had to pay a fee to the King and now a small fee to the Government. Before the water is used for agriculture it is brought up in to small pools so the temperature (which underground is about 50°F) can rise to an ambient level.

Opposite page: A Karez tunnel outside Turpan.

After having walked around one of the Karez that has been opened up for the tourists, we went and had a wine tasting that was interesting. I tasted a white wine, which was a blend of Riesling and Chardonnay. It reminded me of Retsina, a perfectly drinkable Cabernet and another wine that was similar to the Southern French sun-drenched wines, which I felt would give one a head.

later I went around the Turpan Museum, which had a complete skeleton of a Dinosaur that stood 5 meters tall, 9 meters long and weighed an estimated 30 tons. It lived about 24 million years ago. Also in the Museum were some Mummies that had been buried in the Ancient Tombs of Astana and which featured European as well as Mongolian features.

In the evening we went to the Emin Hioja's Tower and Mosque, built in 1777 and 1778 respectively. The Mosque is very disappointing, as it has no ceramic tiles the whole building only has a clay finish.

I had dinner in the People's Square again.

29th May 2006

Opposite page top: Looking out over vineyards from the Emin Hioja Tower.

Opposite page bottom: The Mosque at Emin Hioja.

We drove from Turpan, first to Ürümchi which is a large Industrial town of 2 million population. The road from Turpan was dual carriageway and very good. Initially we drove through the shale desert and then went through some mountains, before coming to the long and very wide Ürümchi plain, which is heavily cultivated with wheat, potatoes and vines.

40 km before Ürümchi we came across an enormous wind farm, which has 680 turbines. On arrival in Ürümchi we went to the Xinjiang Museum, which had a lot of superbly preserved mummies. Another area of the museum showed the culture, clothes, musical instruments, as well as farming implements used by all the different tribes and countries surrounding Xinjiang. These have had an effect on the local customs.

From Ürümchi we went to Kuitun, my one but last stopping point in China.

Below: A wind Farm just before Ürümchi that has 680 turbines.

30th May 2006

Opposite page top:
Sher and me at a lake just before Yining.

Today we drove the 456 km from Kuitun to Yili. Initially the road took us through some very fertile land, fields surrounded by poplar trees. The road was dual carriage for the first 260 km before becoming a good two way road.

About 140 km, just short of Yining, we came to a lake situated at 2,037 metres above sea level, out of which no river flows. It is surrounded by mountains, which were still snow capped. The lake was very blue and by the shoreline there was a herd of wild horses grazing and drinking in the lake. The whole scene has become very pastoral, as the first of the wild flowers were out, including many dandelions.

On the mountain there were fir trees growing up to the snow line. Just over the hill there was an area that very much reminded me of the Alps - green pastures, steep slopes and firs with snow capped mountain tops.

The hotel, although claiming 3 stars, is in need of a good refurbishment.

Opposite page bottom:
Wild horses grazing in a beautiful flower expanse with lake and mountains behind near Yining.

Left:
The lush green fields on the road to Yili.

JUST
BRING
IT!

1st June 2006

Today was a quiet day as there is nothing of note to see in Yining. We first went to see the Yili River Bridge, which was built only 25 years ago. Prior to that, everyone had to cross the river by boat and every year many people drowned. In the height of the summer, children swim and get washed away. This is the only river in China to flow East to West and ends up by flowing in to the Lake Balkhash in Kaskhstan.

Later we went to he People's Park and Zoo. The zoo was really terrible as the animals were in small cages. For example, a tiger had a space of just 6 steps before having to turn and a lion had an even smaller area. They had no greenery. Eagles and hawks were in cages that did not give them space to attempt to fly, basically it was all very cruel.

Left:
The Yili River at Yining.

2nd June 2006

My final drive in China was to Krorbus to cross the Border to Kazakhstan. The formalities took two hours. My Chinese number plate was replaced with my Dubai plate.

I said goodbye to Sher, who was off back to Turpan to pick up a group of Italians and I crossed into Kazakhstan for the next stage of my journey.

Below:
Following a flock of sheep, horses and cattle being driven by nomads on horseback.

Summary of China

How do you summarize a country the size of China, as it is so enormous with many different ethnic, cultural and religious backgrounds?

One thing that came out strong and clear is that the Chinese Government is making great efforts to develop the whole country, as perhaps up until 10 - 15 years ago Western China and Tibet, which predominantly consist of farming land, lagged behind in receiving money to develop their economies.

The Coastal belt from Shanghai inland to Wuhan is obviously very prosperous. You see many expensive cars, nice houses, dual carriageways and continuous farming down the length of the Yangtse valley. The one thing though that struck me most was that you saw virtually no tractors at all. The fields were laboured over by peasant farmers with their backs facing the sun. Hotels were well run and had Internet in the rooms.

The roads were good, except for the area between Yichang up to 120 km short of Chongqing and from Kangding through to Nyinchi in Tibet. However, in fairness, the Government is building new roads in all of these areas, so within a couple of years the road pattern should be excellent. In Tibet there will always be the risk of landslides, due to the instability of the hills and mountains. There is nothing that anyone can do about that. The mountain scenery is stunning and I can envisage that one day (when is another matter) some of the area from Kangding through to Bome could be made in to wonderful skiing areas.

The Tibetans are a very happy and cheerful people, who toil hard to eke a living out of a harsh climate and high altitude. The World always indicates that the people are not happy being part of China, but that I would strongly dispute this, especially over the last fifteen years or so when the Central Government has really tried to remedy the wrongs of the 1950s – 1970s - the anti-religion campaign and the Cultural Revolution - which were obviously far too extreme and defaced many Buddhists Monasteries and historical sites. I am sure this seriously soured relationships, especially as the Dalai Lama had only left the Country in 1959. Today you see many villages that have been or are being built for the poor Tibetans. The Government has spent many millions of Yuan on assisting in rebuilding old and part

Above:
The rolling fields near Yining.

damaged Monasteries and tourist sites. Many Chinese are Buddhists and can now openly worship. The Tibetans are strong worshippers.

Lots of farmers have small tractors and do not necessarily rely upon Yak, oxen, horses or donkeys to do the ploughing. This applies to Xinjiang and Tibet. Both Tibet and Xinjiang have a strong Buddhist and Islamic religious following.

I decided before the journey that I would never eat in a hotel (as the food can so often be re-heated), but instead experience the local cuisine. During my trip through China and Tibet, I had excellent food eaten in all sorts of restaurants that you almost certainly would not have dreamt of stopping at, if you were walking by. I am pleased to say that I never had one upset stomach in my 42 days in China caused by food.

The people, throughout the regions of China I travelled across, could not have been more openly friendly and interested in what I was doing. In a way, this was proven by the response that the Press gave my trip. I think there were eight articles written, as well as one if not two mentions on Television. Bureaucracy is a problem, but everyone tried very hard to be as cooperative as they could be, especially in Shanghai where they were unsure how to deal with many of my requirements with only a short lead time. However, my original letter to Mr. Hu Jintao, The Secretary General of the PR of China, certainly pulled strings.

The trip was arranged by CITS and it could not have gone more smoothly. I am deeply indebted to the seven guides who accompanied me, because they tried desperately hard to give me the information that I requested and saw so many sites that I would never have visited, if I had been on my own. The three best guides were Chua Chen in Chengdu, Tsering in Tibet and Sher in Xinjiang. The others were good, but lacked the local knowledge that the other three had.

Left:
Using by Thuraya satellite telephone to my daughter in Yining, the first time that I had been able to have communication, other than e-mail.

Chapter 3

Kazakhstan

2nd June 2006

I crossed in to Kazakhstan from the Chinese border post at Khorbus.

The clocks are two hours behind China, so although I had lost time on the Chinese Border, I gained it again as soon as I was in Kazakhstan. The Kazakh officials could not have been more helpful and due to the language problem were very patient. They were very interested in the car, which has the Dubai Plates back on again, as I do not think they had seen a Volvo XC 90 before. The border formalities took about an hour and then it was off to Almaty.

The distance from Khorbus to Almaty is 360 km. The first 200 km was through wide open scrub and grasslands, with no person or animal to be seen. We then crossed a small range of hills and started to come in to farmland and villages, where the villages were long and spread out. The police are very strict on speed and have many speed guns. Oncoming motorists flash to warn you. All the houses were single storey, until you came in to Almaty itself, which is a big city built on the side of a hill. Luckily it is laid out very symmetrically, which made it easy to find where you were, once you had your initial location and bearings.

I found the Hotel Zhetisu, but The Travel Agents had not booked a room - in fact they had done nothing even though I had e-mailed three days before, confirming my arrival. Anyway it did not matter, as I booked my room. In the evening walked to the Dublin Bar at the far end of the City and had a reasonable pub dinner and two pints of Guinness.

A restless night as the room was very warm and there were mosquitoes, so today must buy some repellent.

Above:
The Old Parliament Building. The new Parliament is in Astana, the new capital city of Kazakhstan.

3rd June 2006

I walked for miles around Almaty, an interesting City as it has lots of parks and all the streets are tree lined, so coolled the area during the warm days.

There are restaurants and cafes everywhere, so no shortage of choice.

I was going to go and see Faust at the theatre, but had a sleep in afternoon and woke up as the concert was about to start. Dinner was at Stetsons, which was not awfully good. As I walked past the Opera house I heard the music, which sounded very nice.

4th June 2006

Again, I walked for miles and found the Regent Hotel, which had a broadband connection, so I was able to catch up on sending photographs to Omnia in Dubai. On my travels I came upon the Zekhov Cathedral, which is very colourful, but did not go inside as there was a service in progress. Close by the cathedral is the Eternal Flame to remember those killed during the Bolshevik Revolution and Second World War. The gardens here were well looked after and or for a change the grass was cut which is not normally the case. The rose beds were well tended, which is normally the case.

I ate in a good restaurant, Inara, which is popular and serves good shishkababs and an excellent soup. I was interested to see the number of girls there drinking Vodka.

Above:
Statue to two local War heroes that replaced the statue of Lenin in Almaty.

Opposite top:
The Eternal Flame in Almaty.

Opposite bottom:
The Zhenkov Cathedral in Almaty.

5th June 2006

An interesting day of driving. I had originally planned to stay in Taraz, but had to move on to Shymkent, as the traffic police would not let me stay, having stopped me for speeding (which I was not), and as I did not have Kazakh Insurance cover they required $200.00 or local currency 20,000 which is $1500. This all seemed a bit strange, though they were very pleasant, but insisted that I drove on to Shymkent. Within the next 40 km I was stopped three more times for no reason other than for a chat and shake of hands. I think the mobile phones had been busy. The Police were renowned for taking or extracting bribes.

The scenery is enormous and difficult to explain because it is miles upon miles of grasslands with a few rolling hills for as far as the eye can see, until you come to areas that are cultivated with wheat and barley. A few crops were being harvested and the grass being cut and bailed for hay. I passed through very few villages, but saw a lot of cattle and sheep nearer to Shymkent. For the first 200+ km there were few animals.

I stayed at the Hotel Kema, which was quite reasonable and modern. For dinner I had Shishkabab at some restaurant on the street,

Below:
Honey being sold on the Almaty to Taraz road.

which was very good and a nice beer from the Shymkent Brewery - apparently the only thing that Shymkent is renowned for!

6th June 2006

A very quiet day as I had to arrange the local car insurance, which I did after much amusement and time, thanks to the language problems. The staff in the Halyn Insurance, part of Halyn Bank Group, could not have been nicer.

I washed the car and found an Internet Bar. Additionally, I called Uzbekistan to ensure that the guide would be ready for me at the Customs post, as I cross in to Uzbekistan tomorrow.

Had a good meal at a small café of cold vegetable consommé, good mixed salad and chicken.

7th June 2006

I drove to the Tashkent border, 120 km away. The process of crossing was uneventful.

Below:
Wild flowers for as far as the eye could see, alongside the Almaty to Taraz road.

Chapter 4

Uzbekistan

7th June 2006

I was met at the border by my guide to be, Shauket, who was in his late 30s and married with a daughter and son. He helped me through the Customs procedures, which were not onerous and by 10.30am we were finished.

We drove to the office of Asia Travel and en-route we were stopped four times by the police, for no reason. On each occasion, Shauket talked with the police and no money passed hands. Bribes are the name of the day in Uzbekistan, but Shauket said that I had just arrived and was here to raise awareness for blind people. This seemed to do the trick. It was agreed that after lunch we would drive to Samarakand and see Tashkent on the last day. We would find hotels as we went along, seeing that the tourist season was over.

The journey to Samarakand was covered on a good road. We drove through extensive farming land all the way, stopped for a tea, apricots and cherries at a café just after the Tamerlane Gate. All caravans had to pass through the Tamerlane Gate on leaving Samarakand and pay their taxes or dues, some 60 km away. It was similar to the idea of the Yumen Pass in the Gobi Desert, near Dunhuang in China that I had visited on the 25th May.

We stayed at the Zarina Hotel in Samarakand, which was built 10 years ago, but renovated 4 years ago. It was quiet and comfortable and only three minutes walk from the Bibi Khanym Mosque, which was built by Tamerlane's Chinese wife as a surprise for him. The Architect required a kiss from her before he completed the works and as a result Tamerlane ordered that all women should wear a veil. The Architect was murdered.

We dined in a nearby Shishkebab restaurant that was very good.

8th June 2006

Shauket arranged for a local guide to take me around the historical sites. Svetlana is an Uzbek girl, who knew the history of all the sites and was very helpful in her explanations.

Firstly, we visited the Ulughbek Observatory, which was built by Ulughbek in the 1420s and who was probably better known as an

Above:
The Tamerlane Pass, the route which all caravans travelling the Silk Road had to go through and pay taxes.

astrologer rather than Ruler. The observatory was discovered in 1908 and all that was found of the remains was the curved instrument track. From books it shows that the readings of the stars were accurate to within 2 minutes.

From there we went to the Shahr-i-Zindah tombs that are walking distance from the Bibi-Khanym Mosque. The tombs are seen to be some of the most sacred in Samarakand, as the cousin of Prophet Mohamed, Qusam ibn Abbas, is said to be buried there. Qusam ibn Abbas brought Islam to the area. The other main tombs are those of the niece of Tamerlain and Ulughbek's families. Many of the tombs have been restored and there are still enough of the original tiles to see the craftsman's skills compared to the more modern tiles.

Then on to the Bibi-Khanym Mosque, which was finished in 1404 the year before Tamerlane died of pneumonia in Kazakhstan, during one of his military campaigns. The Mosque was commissioned by Tamerlane's Chinese wife as a surprise for her husband and legend

has it that the architect fell in love with her and would not finish the structure, unless she would give him a kiss. Tamerlane returned and heard of the story and is said to have had the architect murdered. The building was seen to be the jewel in his empire, but due to certain design faults, structural problems soon started the building to crumble. It was finally destroyed in an earthquake in 1897. The Uzbek government rebuilt the structure against UNESCO advice and there are already signs of deterioration, but it shows an impressive main gateway with several domes.

Above:
Shauket, my guide in Uzbekistan, awaiting tea and apricots just after passing through the Tamerlane Pass.

We then walked into the Bazaar, which is full of merchants selling anything from fresh bread, fruit, vegetables, spices and nuts from the region. The bazaar is very colourful and is buzzing with activity. The Uzbek ladies wear very colourful dresses.

After lunch we went to the Registan, the first building of which was built in 1420 by Ulughbek as a Madrassa for theology, mathematics, astrology and philosophy teaching. The inner courtyard had 28 rooms for 56 students. The rooms were comparatively large, with an upstairs

Above:
Standing in front of the Registan in Samarakand.

sleeping area. Today, there is glass in the windows, but in those days paper soaked in oil was fixed to the window frames, in winter, to stop the wind, but allow the light in.

In 1636 Shaybanid Emir Yalangtush built a replica of the Ulughbek Madrassa facing on to it and in 1660 the Tilla-Kari, (Gold-Covered) Mosque and Madrassa were built to create the centre of a three-sided square. The walls and dome are painted in gold leaf and are fabulous to look at.

We went in to one madrassa room, which is now a museum displaying all the Uzbek musical instruments. A man played an assortment of the instruments - from a type of xylophone to mandolins, all of which are made from mulberry wood, to a flute and drum/tamberine.

Finally, we visited the Guri Amir Mausoleum where Tamerlane was laid to rest beneath a dark green Jade stone block in a mausoleum that he originally built for two of his sons and two grandsons, as well as Ulughbek. The Mausoleum is hexagonal but from the interior you would think it was square. The lower part of the wall was lined with

onyx and the upper two-thirds and dome were decorated with papier-mâché, painted in gold, blue and yellow and ochre. Altogether there are seven tomb stones inside, as Tamerlane had his most revered teacher, Sheikh Umar, buried there too. Tamerlane consulted Sheikh Umar before every military campaign to agree on the most auspicious time to commence each campaign.

Above:
Svetlana, a local Uzbec guide of Samarakand, in front of the Shahr-in-Zindah tombs.

Opposite:
The Bibi-Khayam Mosque, Samarakand..

Left:
An overloaded donkey in the market in Samarakand.

9th June 2006

We drove to Bukhara via the town from which Tamerlane came, some 100 km ESE of Samarakand. The road took us up over a mountain pass of some 1,800 meters and the view either way was interesting: the rocks on the southern side looked ready to slide given just a slight earthquake.

We arrived at Shakhrisabz, which was first built around 2,700 years ago and is the town where Tamerlain was born in 1334. He started to build a Summer Palace there in 1386, which was completed in 1404. Originally, with the dome it was 70 meters high. However, with what remains of the building either side of main gate is 38 meters high and still has most of its own blue tiles. From the top one has a very good view out across the town and surrounding countryside. In front of the building there is a bronze statue of Tamerlane that was erected 6 years ago and replaced one of Lenin.

Below:
Looking down to Tamerlane's statue from the top of the summer palace in Shahkrisabz.

From there we went to the Mosque that was built by Ulughbek and where there is the empty tomb that Tamerlane built for himself, but was not buried in because he died of pneumonia and meningitis in Kazakhstan in 1405. His body was brought back in a wooden coffin and was buried in Samarakand, as they could not cross the mountain pass, due to a severe winter.

Up to Shakhrisabz, we passed through farming land, chiefly growing wheat and barley. Leaving Shakhrisabz the landscape was much the same, until the last 100 km to Bukhara where the land was semi desert.

Arriving in Bukhara, we stayed at the Lyabi B&B which is a converted Jewish merchant's home and is very comfortable. I found an internet café and was able to upload a few photographs, but the system was desperately slow. In the evening we had dinner in the square opposite and got chatting to a young couple who were hoteliers.

Below:
The doorway to the Ulughbek Mosque in Shahkrisabz.

AMIR
TEMUR

Opposite: Standing in front of Tamerlane's statue, Shahrkrisabz.

10th June 2006

My guide, Gylia, is the top State guide and controls all the registered guides operating in Bukhara. Bukhara City has a population of 270,000 with the district comprising of 1.5 million people. The original settlement was built 2,500 years ago and appears to have been rebuilt about 12 times.

We started off by visiting the Kukeldash Madrassa and Nadir Divanbegi Madrassa, both built in the early 1600s. The Nadir was originally used as a caravanserai. Both were built by Abdul Khan's treasury minister, who financed them.

The streets of the old part of town, especially in the Jewish district, are very narrow. We stayed in the Lyabi Hotel, which was once built and owned by a Jewish trader. In the last 8 years most of the Jews have left Uzbekistan, as the cost of living and quality of life has seriously deteriorated since "Independence". Small, covered bazaars abound in the centre of town and most have four streets leading in to the bazaar itself. Consequently, they are cool, thanks to thick walls and a draught or wind, which keeps the air circulating. Within the bazaars there are people selling rugs, cloth, caps, nicknacks etc. and all are the same, though originally each had its own speciality. A number of new hotels have been constructed, which is spoiling the traditional views of central Bukhara.

We visited the Maghoki-Attar Mosque, which is one of the oldest buildings in Bukhara, the remains of a Buddhist, 5th century Zoroastrian, and a church that was destroyed by the Arabs. In the 16th century the Jews used the mosque as a synagogue.

From there we walke to the blue-tiled Ulughbek Madrassa, which was built in 1417. It is one of three madrassas that Ulughbek built during his reign. Opposite there is the Abdul Aziz Khan's Madrassa built in 1652. All have been restored over the last 100 years to some degree or other. From there we walked down the silk road along which all caravans had to pass and came to the Kalon Minaret and Kalon Mosque - the second largest practicing mosque in Uzbekistan. The Minaret built in 1127 is 47 meters high and has 10 meters of foundations, built on reeds to absorb earthquakes. It has never required major restoration,

Above:
The Bolo-Hauz Mosque with wooden porch of Poplar, Elm and Walnut in Bukhara built in 1718.

even Ghengiz Khan spared it because of its beauty.

The Kalon Mosque was re-opened in 1991 having being restored. It is big enough to hold 10,000 people and has 288 small domes. The original mosque was destroyed by Genghis Khan in the 16th century and the Russians used it as a warehouse.

Opposite the Kalon Mosque is the Mir-i-Arab Madrassa, which is the only madrassa still in use in Bukhara. The madrassa is named after 16th century Naqshbandi Sheikh from the Yemen, who had a strong influence over Shaybanid ruler Ubaidullah Khan. Both are buried under the northern dome.

The Citadel, Ark, was built either in the 1st or 4th century AD. It was lived in by the Ruler of Bukhara from the 5th century until 1920. The last coronation took place in 1910. The Citadel is now a museum and has a 16th century Juma (Friday) mosque that now houses some old manuscripts.

Above:
Madrassa built by Ulughbek in Bukhara.

Behind the Ark is the Bolo-Hauz Mosque, built in 1718. It has a very fine wooden porch and 20 columns made from walnut, elm and poplars. Close by is the Chasma-Ayub Mausoleum where Job was supposed to have stuck his staff into the ground and a spring appeared, providing clean and cool drinking water.

Finally we went to the Turki Jandi Mausoleum, where if you walk around it three times your prayers will be answered. The area used to be a very large graveyard where thousands of skeletons have been found.

In the evening I had dinner with Shauket and two of his friends in an old madrassa. One is a lecturer in metal design carving and his school friend, a shop owner. We watched the England's first World Cup match, which they wanted to watch!

Overleaf:
The Kalon Minaret built in AD 1127 on a 10-foot reed bed and is 47 meters high.

11th June 2006

This morning we drove 13 km from Bukhara to the Bakhatdin Naqshband Mausoleum, in the village of Kasri Orifin. It is one of Sufism's most important shrines and houses the tomb of Bakhautdin Naqshband. It also has the first Ladies Mosque, which has a beautifully carved wooden ceiling.

From there we moved on to the Emir Alim Khan's Summer Palace, known as the Sitoria Mokhi Hosa (Moon and Stars). It is said that this is where Alim Khan had 40 concubines and 20 eunuchs and was unknown to his 4 wives, through whom he had 13 children. The Palace is now a museum of gifts given by the Russians, Chinese and Japanese.

Finally we went to the Chor-Bakr, a 16th century necropolis. It is thought to be associated to Abu-Bakr, a close friend of Prophet Mohamed. A very quiet and peaceful place.

Previous page top:
The Citadel or Ark built in the 4th Century AD and lived in from the fifth Century by the Ruler of Bukhara until 1920.

Previous page bottom:
The only remaining working Madrassa in Bukhara, with 146 students.

Opposite:
The Entrance Hall to the Emir Alim Khan Summer Palace.

Below:
The wooden carved ceiling in the Ladies Mosque in Bakhautdin Naqshband Mosque.

12th June 2006

Above:
The Chasma Ayub Mosque.

We drove to Tashkent on a shorter route than the one we took when heading south. The total distance was 608 km. The car had its first puncture 120 km short of Tashkent. It looks as though a spike got it. Changing the wheel took a few minutes, despite the 36°C heat. A local came and helped, which was kind.

In the five days since going south, the harvest has really got underway and many fields of wheat have been cut. Apricots are available everywhere.

We are staying at the Tashkent Palace Hotel, which is very comfortable and in the heart of the city. The Parliament building, with its fountains in front, is very impressive. Alongside is a park that celebrates and remembers those who were killed in the Second World War with an eternal flame. I then walked via the Art Gallery and Opera House back to the hotel.

Had dinner in the amusement park, which was reasonable.

Opposite top:
The Eternal Flame and memorial to the Second World War dead in Tashkent.

Opposite bottom:
The Parliament Building in Tashkent.

SEN DOIM

13th June 2006

Opposite:
Shauket and his family at a lake outside Tashkent where we went for the day.

Today, we drove to the mountains bordering on Kyrgyzstan, some 100 km East of Tashkent. I took Shauket's wife and two children along with us as well. We went in a chair lift about three km up a hillside, which was pleasant, as there were a few wild horses and lots of wild flowers, lilies etc. to see. From the top one could see the snow-capped mountains in Kyrgyzstan, which form part of the Tianshan mountain range, all the way around to Turpan in China. From there we had lunch next to a very blue reservoir, before driving back along the President's Road, which he had specially built, so he could get to his country home easily!

In the evening I went to watch Faust at the Opera House in Tashkent, which was enjoyable. It lasted 3¾ hours. The singing and music were good, but the scenery was fairly basic and during set changes you could hear the banging of nails. Not quite Covent Garden!

14th June 2006

Having collected the spare tyre that had been repaired I crossed back into Kazakhstan and on to Shymkent. Shauket made sure that everything went smoothly at the border.

Summary of Uzbekistan

My general opinion is that Uzbekistan is very much geared and orientated towards the tourist, compared to Kazakhstan. They have some very beautiful historical buildings, but if they are not careful they may spoil them by building new hotels right in the heart of the City of Bukhara, which has already started to be the case.

The Uzbeks are most friendly, and I had good food, although Shishlak is common.

Chapter 5

Back To Kazakhstan

14th June 2006

I crossed back in to Kazakhstan and drove back to Shymkent. I was delayed at the Kazakh border, because I coincided with lunchtime.

The drive to the town was uneventful, partially, as I learned later, because the police had been stopped from using their radar guns by the government. As a result I did not see one.

In the afternoon I went to the Internet café to catch up on my e-mail. I had a slight jippy tummy, so went to bed early. A little later, I was woken up by an unexpected knock on the door. It was my new guide-to-be, Irina, who would accompany me across Kazakhstan, as had been arranged through Silk Road Adventures in Uzbekistan. Irina wanted the details of our journey for the next day.

15th June 2006

We left Shymkent and drove to Turkistan, a town 170 km to the west, and went around a cluster of sites on the edge of the Kysylkum desert, where Kazakhstan's holist Muslim site can be found.

Irina is a very pleasant Kazakh Russian woman, good-looking, aged 30 and quite extrovert. However, she only knows the history of Southern Kazakhstan, never having travelled West before. She explained that there was little history further west.

The Mausoleum of the first great Turkic Muslim, Kozha Ahmed Yasaui, was built by Tamerlain in the 14th Century. The site is thought to have been established in the 5th Century, but came to its greatest point in the 12th Ccntury, as a trading post.

Yasaui was a Sufi teacher as well as a Turkic poet. He undertook his original teaching in Bukhara, but moved to Turkistan fairly early on. He died in 1166 in his underground cell, where he had retired to, but only came out after dark. Yasaaui's tomb was used as a pilgrimage site and it was Tamerlane who decided to build today's mausoleum.

Close by there is an old Turkish bath which is very nicely laid out in the 15th century style.

There is also the mausoleum of Rabigha-Sultan Begum, the wife of Abdul-Khayir Khan, who was killed in 1468. His death effectively divided the Uzbeks from the Kazakhs.

Right:
The Turkic Muslim Kozha Ahmed Yasaui Mausoleum in Turkistan.

The last mosque was the Hal-Wat Mosque, which was built underground and where Yasaui is meant to have retired to.

Right:
The Bath House built in the 15th century in Turkistan.

16th June 2006

I decided that we would drive to Aral'sk in one go, provided the road was in good enough condition, which luckily it was - a distance of 787 km. The scenery was rolling plain / steppes the whole way, though initially grassland until after Kzyslorda when it became corn and reeds. The last 300 km was a landscape very similar to that of Dubai's scrub and low dunes, but every so often watering holes where camels, horses and cows would be watering.

We arrived in Aral'sk, which really looked like a downtrodden town. Eventually, we found the hotel, which was the only one in town. Although it was run down, it was clean and the receptionist was helpful. Shortly after arrival, we went four doors away to arrange for a guide to show me around the Aral Sea the next day. I had been longing to see the sea, due to the reported catastrophic decline in the lake's water levels, following the Russian desire to grow cotton. 100 yards from the hotel is the old port which has 4 ships up on stocks as a museum, two dilapidated cranes with a small streak of water and in the distance other rusting hulks. There was virtually no water to be seen.

The hotel, called the Aral Hotel, must have last seen a paint brush 15 years ago. It was totally dilapidated, but at least had a bed. The receptionist was the only person who was helpful.

Today's temperature was 37°C.

Below:
Camels grazing on the steppes, which stretch for hundreds of miles and are as barren as can be seen here.

Above:
The Aral Hotel that probably last saw a paint brush 15 years or more ago.

17th June 2006

I met up with the guide, Ceric, and we went off to see the remnants of the Aral Sea. Ceric was 23 and until the year 2000 had never seen the Aral Sea himself, as it had disappeared completely from the town of Aral'sk. in the 1970s. He now works for an organisation, in part sponsored by the Israelis and Danes, trying to re-train the Aral'sk folk to a new way of life, as well as training a few in fish farming and the control of the fish stock.

The Israelis pulled out of the project, as the people being trained would not devote all their time, care and attention to the various projects, or the government would not support continuity after the initial training. They planted 2,500 trees, installed an irrigation system on the edge of town, but the local government would not provide the money for the electricity for use in irrigation in the summer. Now there are less than 600 small trees left.

In 2003, the Russians built a barrier 12.8 km long across a narrow strip of the Aral Sea, in order to divide it in to two. The Northern Sea is what is now called the Little Aral and the Southern, the Big Aral Sea, which

is, ultimately, expected to dry up. In the Little Aral Sea, Denmark has set up a fish hatchery farm that was planned to introduce 12 million flounders and catfish in to the sea a year, so that they could rebuild the fishing industry to some extent. The hatchery is now producing only 6 million hatchlings, as they will not, or have not, the money to pay for the heating in the winter, when everything freezes over.

In 2003, the Northern Aral Sea was 62 miles away from the town of Aral'sk, but after the building of the dam it was by 2016, only 12 miles away. As a result, the climate has changed, bringing clouds and a reduction in the salinity of the water. It is hoped that Aral'sk will once again have the sea water back in the harbour within a few years.

The initial dam built by the Russians breached its walls as the structure was not robust enough. We drove 240 km to the new barrier that is 12.6 meters high and paid for by a World Bank loan. They have installed a flood gate to allow excess water to be fed in to the Big Aral, but did not take account of the fact that fish will be lost through the sluices as the water flows out. Indeed we saw fishermen pulling fish

Above:
Looking across what used to be Aral'sk Port in the middle can just be seen the two quayside cranes.

Opposite top:
Two fishing boats retained as a memorial to the days when Aral'sk was a fishing port landing over 100,000 tons of fish a year.

Opposite bottom:
Looking across what was once Aral'sk Port and now a museum showing the port, cranes and fishing boats.

ПТС Лев Берг

out below the sluice gates and selling to Shymkent.

The drive for the first 90 km was on the main Kyzlorda to Aral'sk road and thereafter by dirt road 120 kilometers to the barrier. We passed three lakes that are completely unaffected by the Sea's activities and these were deep blue, reflecting the sky. There were reeds around the edge and cattle, horses and camels grazing, as well as providing fishing. I also saw many eagles swooping for rodents. We twice crossed the Syr Darya River, which feeds the Sea.

Aral'sk otherwise has nothing to offer. It is like a ghost town, despite the 38,000 people living there.

Below:
Fishermen hauling in nets just below the overflow from the small Aral Sea that is slowly filling since the building of a dam, funded by the World Bank.

Above:
The Syr Darya River that feeds the Little Aral Sea.

18th June 2006

Today we drove the 645 km to Aktobei. It turned out to be a rather disastrous day though, as after the first 150 km along a good road, the tarmaccame to an abrupt end. From smooth running, we went on to a dirt road, the main highway, for the next 250 km. It could not really be described as a road, as it either had enormous potholes anything up to 24 inches deep, or sections of deep ruts. Sadly, I hit one pothole hard and damaged the front left shock absorber, which at the time I did not realise. When I jacked the car up as I saw a spring sitting on top of the tyre. So I took the wheel off, shook the shock absorber about and put the wheel back on. There was now a small clearance, so I was able to proceeded slowly onwards. After 75 kilometers I had a blow-out, due to the tyre being worn through to the wire. I changed the wheel and carried on for another 120km when the same thing happened yet again! Once more I changed the wheel, but this was my last spare and still had 100 km to go. We finally arrived finally Aktobei at 8.00 pm. With great relief that we had got there, we booked in to a hotel and then went for a much needed beer and soft drink for Irina.

Irina spoke to a man at the next table to see if he would know of a garage where we could have the car repaired. He immediately pulled out his mobile phone and said someone would come to the hotel at 8.00am the next morning.

19th June 2006

At 8.00am a person called Telman arrived and it turned out that he was the younger brother of the person that we met the previous night. We were then told that the elder brother was the Aktobei Regional Police General, Atab Kojshin, and very powerful in the City. He had instructed his brother to ensure that everything was done to repair the car and to look after us.

Telman took us to his garage and after the front wheels were taken off we could see that the right front shock absorber was bent. We were taken off to various car supply depots, but were unable to find a new shock absorber. So they set about straightening the old one and we bought five new tyres, which were Russian, and then took the car out to make sure the steering was running true.

In the evening I bought dinner for the General, Telman and another police officer. Poor Irina really worked overtime! We talked non-stop, with Irina translating.

After a while, I realised that the General was suspicious of me

Below:
The main highway from Aral'sk to Aktobei.

and he suspected that I was a spy, as apparently foreigners do not cross Kazakhstan on their own for pleasure. We were told that we should not go to Ural'sk as the road is not good, but cross by another route in to Russia. Telman would lead the way the next morning. I said that this was not possible as my passport showed that I was to cross in to Russia via Ural'sk, but the General insisted that I must cross in to Russia via the route he had ordered.

20th June 2006

We set off at 8.00am to the Border, which was 100 km from Aktobei. However, as I had anticipated, we were not allowed to cross out of Kazakhstan as the Carnet showed that I was going to cross the border at Ural'sk. After a lot of discussion I was not permitted to leave, so we had a wasted journey and returned to Aktobei for the night.

I was now concerned about proceeding on my own, knowing that the car had the shock absorber problem. Irina managed to find a new guide, Dan, to take me up to Moscow. He happened to be a Kazakh

Below:
The rutted main highway to Ural'sk.

Lawyer by training and had studied in the USA and Moscow, but was currently working in the Tenghis Oil Fields as an Administrator. He was 29 years old and on a 20 days holiday, besides, he could do with some extra cash. Dan, Irina and I had a good dinner together.

21st June 2006

Dan and I set off at 8.30am for Ural'sk, slightly in trepidation of what was in front of us as the distance was 475 km and we had been warned that a fair section of the road was not good.

Sure enough there was 250 km of bad road, but I must say, not as bad as the Aral to Aktobei stretch. This is a main International Highway - well actually, some of it was purely a sand road. It was often better to run along the soft hard shoulder than drive on the carriageway, as on the hard surface you often could not see the deep holes until you were virtually on top of, or in, them. We discovered the tell-tale sign was that was if a track has been created on the hard shoulder that means there was a major pothole in the middle. Anyway the car stood up well.

Below:
Dan and his girl friend Sultana and I having a drink in Ural'sk.

The last 140 km was on good tarmac, but I kept the maximum speed down to 100km/h as I did not want any more problems.

On arrival in Ura'lsk we found a nice hotel, arranged car insurance for Russia and filled up ready for the next morning's crossing to Russia and Samara. I found a good Internet connection where I was able to up load photographs for the website.

In the evening I took Dan and his girlfriend Sultana out to dinner which was very pleasant, as she also spoke good English.

22nd June 2006

We have just 59 km to go to the Russian Border. We left the hotel at 8.30am and arrived about 45 minutes later to queue to get in to the Border Post. This took nearly one hour and when we did finally get into Russia, we were told that we could not cross that point as the Russians did not handle Carnets. So we had to return to Ural and head towards the border at Sarotov a further 118 km away.

About 20 km short of the Border Post the shock absorber

Below:
Looking out over the steppes on the road to Ural'sk.

went again. We managed to hobble to the border and after awaiting another hour the Customs men recommended that we should get the car repaired in a village 20 km back down the road, as they could not advise us to go to Russia like this. Once again we retraced our path and off we went to find the garage which would hopefully be able to repair and strengthen the shock absorber. Next door to the garage was a small café, so we had a belated lunch.

The garage owner was a very pleasant person and said he could repair the shock absorber and ensure that we were able to reach Moscow, 3,000 km away, which is where the nearest Volvo workshop was. In the course of heating the shock absorber he managed to over-heat it and all the oil blew out! With an effectively useless shock absorber, the only repair the mechanic was able to achieve was to weld a rod along the length of the shock absorber, keeping it at an even height when fitted to the car. He said that it was safe to drive, although at every bump that we drove over there would be a noise of metal on metal and that we should not travel at more than 90 km/h.

Below:
The car shock absorber being repaired for the second time, 20km short of the Russian border.

We drove back to the border with the shock absorber making a pretty awful sound. Once again, we queued for entry into Russia. After a further hour, the documents were finally stamped and every item in the car was inspected by a Customs Officer. He informed us that we had filled in the declaration form incorrectly, but that he would let us go, if we paid him 500 roubles. I gave him a Classical Music CD instead!

At last we crossed in to Russian Customs at 7.00pm Russian time (8.00pm Kazakh time).

Conclusion

Kazakhstan is an enormous country with little scenery along my route, other than the Steppes. I am told that to the East and North there are mountains, which are apparently very beautiful, but I only saw some near to Almaty.

The Kazakhs, on the whole, were not as friendly as the Uzbeks and certainly do not go out of their way to welcome the tourist. However, that might be about to change as the Government has stopped the

Below:
The garage where the shock absorber was repaired.

police from pulling vehicles over at their will and extorting bribes for made up traffic offences. General Kojshin said that he took the action that he did, because of the new directive of helping tourists.

The roads are not good, especially the road from Aral'sk to Ural'sk. This must damage the economy, as one has to drive so slowly, but work is underway to repair the road. That said, I believe the road foundations are not as solid as they should be to prevent the heavy lorries from continuing to break up the surface. One could see signs, even on recently laid surfaces, of holes developing.

I am glad that I have travelled across the country, because beforehand I had not appreciated the size of the Kazakhstan. It has enormous petroleum and gas wealth, which is just beginning to be exploited and should allow for the development of the infrastructure - so long as corruption can be properly and effectively controlled.

I also passed by, but in the far distance, the Baikanour Cosmodrome, which the Russians use for their flights to the International Space Station.

Chapter 6

Russia

22nd June 2006

Opposite top:
The Yershov War Memorial for the Second World War.

Dan and I drove up to the Russian Customs point, where we had to wait about 30 minutes before Passport Control was completed. However, it took another hour to get the Carnet finally, approved as the Russian Federation do not really recognise it. As always, everyone was very friendly and eventually at 8.30pm, Russian time, we were in Russia.

The next question was, where were we going to stay? I decided we would go approximately 150 km from the border. At the first village we filled up with fuel, but there was no hotel and the people did not seem friendly, so we drove on a further 50 km to Yershov, arriving at 10.45 pm. We found a hotel, referred to in a local mini market, as the Pentagon, but it was in fact the Railway hotel, opposite the station. The rooms were clean, but sparse and without a shower. We were told of a house where we could park the car safely, so I took it there. This was a house owned by an Azerbaijani. In the store we bought some bread, cheese and sausage for supper, whilst the hotel lady made tea.

I fell in to bed really quite tired, but relieved that we had finally left Kazakhstan on the third attempt. The road in Russia was still uneven and so the poor shock absorber was still suffering. God willing, tomorrow we will find a proper major road.

That was certainly a day to remember.

The scenery in Russia was absolutely flat and heavily cultivated.

23rd June 2006

Opposite bottom:
Standing outside the station and War Memorial at Yershov.

I woke up early, as there were too many mosquitoes and despite having sprayed them, they kept re-appearing. I collected the car from the Azerbaijani's house and updated the diary. We then set off at 8.00am.

Dan, so far, has been excellent and without his help I do not know how I would have managed. We set off towards Saratov and hoped to reach Penza by the evening.

The car seemed ok and although the road was rough and there was a lot of noise coming from the shock absorber, all seemed to be well, when we were travelling on a good surface, the noise virtually disappeared. We passed by enormous fields of corn, potatoes and other crops. The first 250 km was completely flat with few villages to see. We

РШОВ

arrived at Saratov, 200 km from Yershov and walked round the city for a while, before carrying on towards Penza.

We were stopped 3 times by the traffic police to check our papers. The first two were uneventful, but on the third occasion, knowing I had done nothing wrong, the policeman decided to breathalyse me and said I had alcohol. This was not possible, because I had not had a drink for two days and the day before that, only one beer. They wanted to drive me the 100 km back to Saratov to have a blood sample taken. The policeman also wanted US$1,000 from me, which was then lowered to US$500. Dan told the policeman that I did not have that amount of cash, other than in Travellers Cheques. He eventually settled on $100 and we were allowed to proceed. Another worrying moment!

Below:
Looking at the bridge that we are about to cross over the Volga River to Saratov.

We eventually arrived in Penza, which seemed to be a really nice country town with pleasant old buildings. Everyone was very friendly, except the traffic police who appear to be after everyone.

I went to the Bank to change a traveller's cheque and it was as though this has never occurred before, because three girls got involved in the transaction. After 30 minutes I got the money much to the sigh of relief of the people queuing behind us.

Originally, I had planned on travelling from Penza to Kazan in Tatarstan and then via Nizhny Novgorod on to Moscow as Kazan was famous for its 16th century Kremlin that is a World Heritage site, but I decided to bypass this because of the shock absorber.

*Below:
Dan looking nervously at a bull next to the road to Penza, where we had stopped for a sandwich.*

24th June 2006

Opposite top:
St. Basil's Cathedral in Red Square, Moscow. In the foreground an area is being prepared for a concert.

We drove from Penza to Moscow via Ryazan, which was an uneventful journey across a distance of 660 km. The journey was, once again, through large open fields, all under cultivation, as well as various woodland/forest areas. We booked in to the Izmailovo Hotel, which was an enormous complex of four hotels just inside the ring road and within walking distance of the metro.

Left:
Ryazan from the hotel room.

25th June 2006

We spent most of the day sight-seeing around the Red Square area of Moscow, having left the car at the hotel and taking the Metro into the city centre. Red Square is looking very much cleaner and smarter than I remembered from my last visit in 1968, it was a lovely day and we walked miles which Dan was not used to, but he knew Moscow from when he was a student there.

Opposite bottom:
The Cathedral of Christ the Saviour in Moscow.

We saw the wonderful St. Basil's Cathedral which is situated at the end of Red Square.

INTERCESSION CATHEDRAL (ST. BASIL'S)

26th June 2006

Dan arranged for the car to be serviced by the Volvo Agent and to have the front shock absorbers changed. There was heavy thunder at 12.00 noon and the afternoon was very humid. It did not take long for the roads to be flooded, so I waited in the hotel for a call to say the car was repaired.

Dan was to leave today, by train, back to Aktobei. He has been most helpful and managed to overcome most of the police incidences. A very good and cheerful young companion, whose company I thoroughly enjoyed.

27th June 2006

A driver came at 9.00am to take me to collect the car from the Volvo agency. He drove like Michael Schumacher, but we got to the garage safely. The car was not ready, so I had to wait 2 hours, finally taking it back at 12 noon. I drove back to the hotel. Volvo would not pay for the repaired shock absorber, but paid for the other one. They said that I needed 4 new tyres as the ones that I had bought in Aktobei,

Below:
Red Square, looking towards Lenin's mausoleum.

although new, were not good. I said that they were Russian tyres, but they said that they were not good quality and I needed European ones. I therefore agreed to change them, but after 15 minutes they told me that they did not have any in stock. I replied that I would change them in Gothenburg (the home of Volvo) when I get there. It was nice to have a silent car again!

In the afternoon I went down to Red Square via the Metro, which is very clean. The stations each have their own tiled theme and the Metro is well controlled.

Whilst walking down towards the River Volga and the Ministry of the Interior, a man who was walking in front of me dropped a bundle of money from his pocket. I carried on walking and then another person from behind called out and told me to stop. He said that he was a policeman and tried to accuse me of attempting to steal the money. He asked me to empty out my pockets. Luckily I only had 100 roubles actually on me, as well as my passport. He inspected it and eventually let me carry on my way. Moscow, I only found out later, is renowned for this kind of crime and potential robbery.

Below:
The shock absorber that Volvo would not pay for, as it had been repaired. You see the iron rod that was welded on in Kazakhstan.

Above:
A view down the Moskva River in Moscow, looking towards the Interior Ministry.

28th June 2006

I walked around Moscow for five hours, walking for miles. There was lots to see, as you see so much more by walking. I bought the 2006 Norton Anti Virus for my laptop, as my previous licence had run out after six months. Otherwise it was a quiet day and I did nothing, except rest.

In the afternoon, I walked along the Moskva River and saw Peter the Great's Statue, which is enormous. Also of note was the beautiful Christ the Saviour Church, which really glistened in the sunlight.

29th June 2006

Again, I went sight seeing today. The one thing that strikes me about Moscow is how much building work is going on, as well as the refurbishment and painting of buildings. It is also interesting to see the difference between the over and under 40s. The over 40s do not smile and are still stuck in the Soviet era impoliteness, whereas the younger

Opposite:
Peter the Great's statue in Moscow's Moskva River.

Pelm
100
TERRANOVA
ЗОЛОТО
АЛТЫН
26.87 26.95
34.02 34.08
Золотая
БОЧКА

Opposite:
Arbat Street in Moscow. A pedestrian street full of restaurants.

are smartly dressed and generally happy. Police are everywhere. The Metro is a good transit system, clean and efficient, but let down by the staff, who are not courteous.

I can well see why Moscow has gained the reputation of being the most expensive City in the world - 100 roubles does not buy anything. Parking in the hotel cost 350 roubles a night.

30th June 2006

I walked around Moscow again today. Luckily the weather has been really good.

During the day I went in to a hotel near the Bolshoi Theatre to ask where I could book a table for a traditional Russian dinner. The receptionist, who could not have been more helpful, suggested the Gudonov Restaurant adjacent to Red Square. The receptionist was in her 20s, so I asked her why the older Muscovites were so cold and unwelcoming? She said, without hesitation, "they are Soviets and it will take another generation to overcome the problem."

I met up with an old family friend from Dubai, Liz Macgillivray, who was visiting Moscow for 24 hours on behalf of Novartis for whom she worked. We had an excellent dinner at the Gudonov. Liz was the only person I met throughout the whole journey, who I knew before.

Below:
Liz Macgillivray in Red Square.

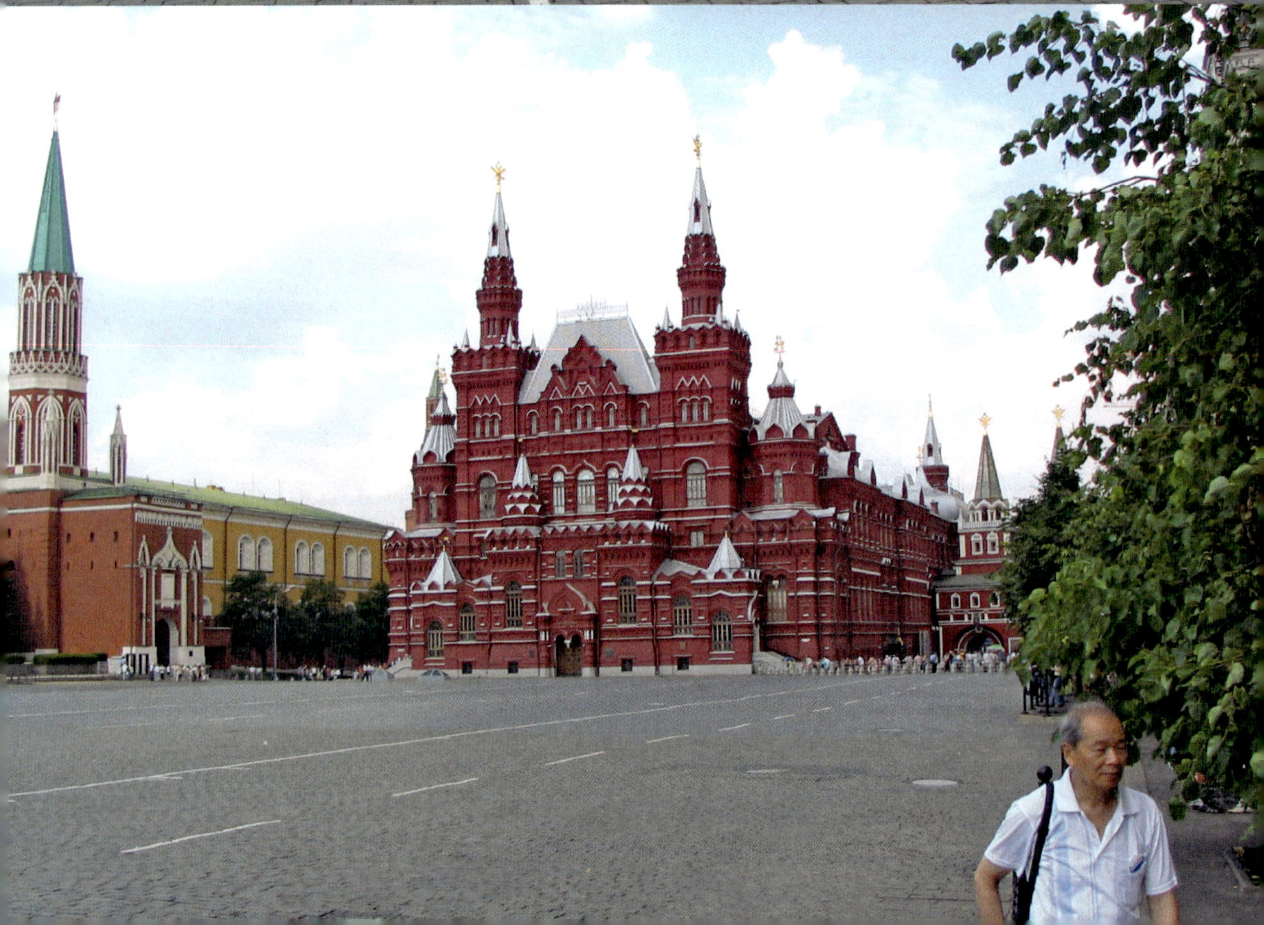

Opposite top:
Red Square looking towards St Basil's Cathedral.

Opposite bottom:
Red Square looking towards the State Historical Museum.

1st July 2006

Today, I drove the 737 km straight to St. Petersburg. The journey was fairly monotonous, as there was little scenery of note. yet again, it was relatively flat, with a lot of birch and pine woods. The road was alright, but certainly not what you would imagine a main highway to be. It was only the last 120 km that had dual carriageway, but that disappeared as soon as a crossroads appeared. There was a lot of construction of new roads, but most of them will end up being three lanes wide, but well signed, as to who has right of way in the centre lane.

I was stopped for speeding, but in an area that did not show a village speed sign. A pleasant young policeman, who spoke some English, settled on a thousand rouble fine and then let me go.

I arrived in St Petersburg and found the apartment that I had rented at US$75.00 a night, which I think was a good rate and only two streets back from the River Neva. It was a ten-minute walk to the Winter Palace. The apartment had a fully furnished kitchen, sitting room and large bedroom. I went to a restaurant just along the street, called Da Vinci, which produced an excellent Italian dinner.

Below:
Palace Square in St. Petersburg.

2nd July 2006

Opposite:
The Spire of Peter and Paul Cathedral on a small island in the River Neva in St. Petersburg.

I walked all over the City, starting by going to the River Neva and then crossing the river to the Maritime Museum with the two Rostal Columns, Neva and Volkhov standing in front. Tourist buses were everywhere. Next, I went to the Peter and Paul Cathedral that has a very high and slim spire, which stands out from miles away, as it is gilded and, in the sunshine, really shone. From there went to the Military Museum and crossed the Neva by another bridge to visit the Eternal Flame, with the Cathedral of the Spilled Blood in the background.

I approached the Cathedral of the Spilled Blood, but being a Sunday, I did not go inside. It has the many coloured domes, like St Basil in Moscow. Following the streets and the canals, I came to the Winter Palace. I happened to enter down a side road that led straight in to the centre of the square. There in the middle of the square was the Alexander Column. The square is enormous with buildings on three sides, all in good condition.

Below:
The Alexander Column in the middle of the Palace Square in front of the Hermitage Museum, which is within the Winter Palace.

Opposite:
One of the two Rostal Columns in on the bank of the River Neva in St. Petersburg.

I bought a ticket into the Winter Palace for 450 roubles and then walked around the rooms, which surely have to be home to one of the best art collections in the world. Many of the rooms are beautiful with painted ceilings etc.. I bought a DVD of the palace, as I could not take it all in and remember everything that I saw.

I saw one of the Bezelik Wall Murals that I had visited at Bezelik in China, only to find that the murals were originally taken to Berlin, but during World War II, the majority were destroyed by Allied bombs. A few were rescued and repaired, after the war, by the Russians, and are now on show in the Hermitage. The Babushka (Museum Lady) would not allow me to take photographs, even though I had tried to explain that I had seen the other murals only six weeks ago, when I visited the site from where these murals originated.

In the afternoon I went on a one-hour boat trip along the canals, which was actually was not as interesting as I thought it would be. The reason was that the water level is about three meters below the road level, so you only see the top of buildings!

In the evening I went to a Greek restaurant, which was great and very busy. Darkness hardly falls at this time of the year, being so far north.

Right:
The Eternal Flame, or Monument To The Fighters of The Revolution, with the Cathedral of the Spilled Blood in the background.

Opposite:
Standing in front of the Church of the Resurrection.

3rd July 2006

Another day of sight-seeing today and I walked many miles and found some lovely buildings in the back streets of St. Petersburg. Later I went around the Russian Museum, which has some lovely paintings, all by Russian artists.

For supper I, again, went to the Greek restaurant.

Below:
The statue of Peter The Great to the west of the Admiralty Building.

Opposite:
The Admiralty in St. Petersburg. All main roads lead directly to the Admiralty.

4th July 2006

I left St. Petersburg at 8.30 am and found my way to the border with no difficulty, crossing over at 12.00 noon. Once again, I had difficulties in getting the Carnet signed off.

Conclusion

I am sad to say that I still find Russia to be oppressive and definitely a police state. You can run in to trouble for no apparent reason. I even dare to say trumped up offenses can be brought against you, especially if you are in a foreign vehicle, but you can buy your way out. This is not a good advertisement for Russia.

St Petersburg is still a totally different city to Moscow, as the people are generally friendly and helpful, whereas in Moscow they are cold and impersonal. This is so sad, as they have much to show the visitor.

I was very surprised by the bad condition of most of the roads. In total drove 2,505km from border to border.

The other thing I noticed was how uncomfortable all the beds were. Indeed, in the Ismailova Hotel the bed was too short and my feet touched the foot board as well as my head touching the headboard. When they make up a bed, they leave the top sheet for you to lay.

The total distance driven in Russia was 2,505 Kilometers.

Below:
The statue of Tsar Nicholas I in St. Isaac's Square.

Chapter 7

Finland

4th July 2006

I crossed in to Finland with no problems and decided to head straight to Jyvaskyla, rather than going via Helsinki and Lathi. The distance to Jyvaskyla was 218 km through continuous spruce and pine forests, with an occasional village and small farms.

Jyvaskyla seems to have changed enormously since 1968, when I was last there. The people were all very friendly and helpful. I explored the city and stayed at the Soroz Hotel which was very nice.

Below:
The Church in Jyvaskyla.

Above:
Oulu Harbour and the red brick warehouses, from where the pine resin tar was exported for ship caulking.

5th July 2006

I moved on to Oulu, a distance of 351 km, again through forests of spruce and pine, passing by many lakes, which are very beautiful.

I stayed at the Hotel Cumulus, which was comfortable. The city is most attractive, sitting on the Gulf of Finland, though you cannot see great expanses of water, just inlets with a small harbour that during the 18th / 19th Centuries was the heart of the pine tar trade to Europe for the caulking of ships. The greatest amount of tar shipped in any one year was 85,000 barrels. The UK was one of the largest buyers. Today, Nokia have a very large centre in the town.

The locals crowded the three bars / restaurants down on the waterfront, which adjoin the market place, to take in as much sun as they could - whilst supping a lot of beer. I had a couple of pints.

Above:
The warehouse where the Pine Tar for caulking boats was stored, prior to shipping It is now part of a museum.

6th July 2006

I drove to Rovaniemi, a distance of 222 kms, again through continuous pine and spruce forests, but with fewer lakes to be seen. It was nice to see some of the hay being dried in the traditional old way, on stakes.

Upon arrival in Rovaniemi, I went 6 km further north to the Arctic Circle and The Santa Claus Village. The village is a dream for the marketer, as they have a captive market of people, who fly to the town to visit Santa Claus and therefore buy the nick-nacks, many of which apparently come from China! The Post Office offers to send cards either immediately or in time for Christmas. Naturally, I got taken in for the latter and will wait to see what arrives.

I booked in to the City Hotel, which is in the centre of town, and then walked for miles around, before having my hair cut. The temperature was 22°C and yet again bright sunshine.

Opposite top:
The car and I have reached the Arctic Circle in Rovaniemi.

Opposite bottom:
A view across the lake to Rovaniemi Church.

NAPAPIIRI
ARCTIC CIRCLE
VOLVO
B DUBAI 23258
XC90

7th July 2006

This morning I drove to Ivalo, 290 km away from Rovaniemi. It was an uninteresting drive, as the scenery was all forest and lakes, although some of the scenes were very attractive.

Some 10% of Finland comprises of lakes, with 73% of the land being forest. The balance is split between towns and farmland.

I stayed in Ivalo, which is really a one man town with nothing of note. At 11.40pm the sun was still up. I ate dinner in the hotel and the entertainment was Karaoke, which was monopolised by two women who were not very good!

Above:
A farm with baled hay, a lake in the background.

Opposite top:
The exciting main street to Ivalo.

Opposite bottom:
Reindeer grazing along the roadside.

HOTEL

8th July 2006

Above:
The sun still up at 11.40pm.

I drove 140 km to the crossing into Norway, which is non-existent, except for the Customs signs. I was originally meant to have stopped in Karasjork for the night, but decided to move on, as I arrived there at 10.30am. I had decided to go straight to Nordkapp, a distance of 440km from Ivalo. The weather was good and very little traffic, so I arrived there at 1.30pm.

Conclusion

Opposite:
The village of Karasjork, the Finnish border town with Norway.

Finland is a beautiful country with absolutely charming and friendly people, but other than for the scenery, there is not a lot to see other than in Helsinki, the capital.

Finland is a country that is expanding fast now that it is no longer under the influence of the Soviet Union.

Skiing, dog-sledding and reindeer treks are really for the spring months, once the sun rises above the horizon. In the summer and in the north of the country there is the 24 hours of sun.

Chapter 8

Norway

8th July 2006 (continued from Finland)

Having crossed over from Karasjork I drove up to Nordkapp passing through some lovely countryside. On the road to Lyuaske came across this beautiful little church in the tiny village of Kistrand, where the Porsanger Fjord begins to widen on its way to the Barents Sea to the east of Nordkapp.

Below:
The beautiful small church at Kristrand, a third of the way up the eastern side of the Porsanger Peninsular, overlooking the Porsanger Fjord.

Overleaf:
Two pictures of the sheer drop of 307 metres (1,007 feet) to the sea at the North Cape.

On approaching Nordkapp, I had to go through four tunnels, the longest of which was 6.8km long, with another of 4 km. Nordkapp is quite expensive to get in to as the toll for the tunnels was €20.00 and the entrance to Nordkapp itself €27.00. The drive was interesting, as there are no trees or bushes - just rock, grass and marshes - and the road winds up and down with sheer drops on one side, in places, with no barriers. There are reindeer grazing and masses of lakes and small rivulets on the banks, where some people were fishing.

The Nordkapp reception centre is very well laid out with a cinema, which takes you all over the area by plane and submarine. It almost made one feel queasy. There is even a small Museum donated by the King of Siam, following his visit there in 1908.

Outside, the metal globe monument in the shape of the world is there with the latitude of North 71°10'21 marked upon it - the furthest North one can travel on land in mainland Europe. The temperature was 17°C, but virtually everyone was wrapped up in an anorak. The sheer 307 metres drop of the cliffs really makes one realise that you are at the end of the world. The next land due northwards is Alaska, some 2,500 miles away.

Below:
The metal globe at Nordkapp, standing at 71°10'21.

Opposite top:
A showcase at the Nordkapp Reception Hall.

Opposite bottom:
Reindeer at Nordkapp.

From there I went and visited a small fishing village called Gerasaerk, which was typically Norwegian with the painted houses and fishing boats moored in the harbour. Most attractive, clean and tidy. *En route* I passed quite a few reindeer grazing along the roadside. I had not previously noticed how large their webbed feet are.

Right:
The village and harbour at Gerasaerk.

Right:
The village of Gerasaerk.

Finally, I travelled on to Honningsvag and stayed at the Rica Hotel, which is on the waterfront in another attractive village.

Left:
Honningsvag, where ocean liners moor on their way around the fjords.

Left:
A cruise liner leaving the Port of Honningsvag.

10th July 2006

I drove 409 km from Alta to Tromsø.

Firstly, I went to the Alta Museum and saw the Rock Paintings, which were carved in to the flat rocks. Although they were etched, the Norwegians painted them in ochre so that they stood out. This was the same pigment colour as used during the early Christian rock paintings. Some of these paintings are believed to be about 6,000 years old.

In the museum, there are also descriptions of the copper mining that started here in the early 1800s. There are also pictures and artefacts of the German Bismark-class battleship, Tirpitz, that was moored for quite a long time in Altafjord, until the allied bombed and damaged it.

The road wound along the fjords with a strict speed limit, which meant it took quite a long time to get to Tromsø. However, the scenery was very beautiful with the high, mostly flat topped, mountains running down to the fjord, with numerous villages and small hay fields, a few cows and sheep.

I stayed at the SAS Radisson hotel in Tromsø and decided to change my date for arriving back in the UK until the 28th July.

Below:
The rock paintings at Alta.

11th July 2006

Opposite:
A statue of a steelworker. Steel made Norway important to Germany in the Second World War.

Today I moved on to Narvik, 250 km from Tromsø.

I visited the War Museum, which is very well laid out and explained the attack on Narvik by the Germans, the intervention of the Allies and the occupation until 1944. I also visited the cemetery and saw the graves of the British forces killed during this period. The cemetery is beautifully laid out and maintained.

Staying at the Quality Hotel, I also had dinner there. I asked one of the waitresses what there was to do in the town after dinner and she said that I could take the cable-car up the mountain, behind the hotel, as it was still open due to the midnight sun.

I duly headed for the cable car station and rode the cable-car as far as it would go. When I got out I could see people walking to the top of the mountain, so off I set. I arrived at the top at about 11.00pm and sure enough, the sun was out. The 360 degrees view was wonderful. I took many photographs, but it was not until I had up loaded the photographs on to my laptop that I noticed the sun reflected in the fiord looked like a duck. I arrived back at the hotel just before midnight.

Below:
Looking down to the town of Narvik from the top of the mountain. The sun's reflection in the fjord resembles a duck.

12th July 2006

A long drive of 762 km to Steinkjer and it rained virtually all day. The views were not good, so I decided not to stay in Moesjoen, as planned.

I stayed at the Quality Hotel Grand and had a very good dinner in a small restaurant outside of the hotel.

Above:
Looking back to Narvik and the ski slopes. I walked to the top of the hill just before midnight. The cable-car went to the top of the ski slopes.

13th July 2006

On to Trondheim this morning, travelling 111 km from Steinkjer. The weather was better, so I arrived in Trondheim at 10.00am, but was too early for the hotel. So I explored the the town.

The waterfront has all the old warehouses converted into offices and apartments. They are painted in different colours which, makes for a colourful scene. The 18th Century wooden Royal Palace in the centre of the town is set right on the street front, whilst the cathedral is considered to be the most important church in Norway, as Trondheim was first established in AD 900 and was the capital of Norway, until Oslo took over. The Cathedral dates back, in part, to the 13th century and is still used for all coronations. The Cathedral has the most beautiful stained glass windows. The Bishops Palace also is 13th century, but became an armoury, until being returned to the church in the late 1560s.

I discovered a little microbrewery tucked in the back streets and enjoyed a couple of good pints.

All of Norway appears to be very clean and no rubbish being dropped by anyone.

Below:
The old warehouses in Trondheim converted to flats.

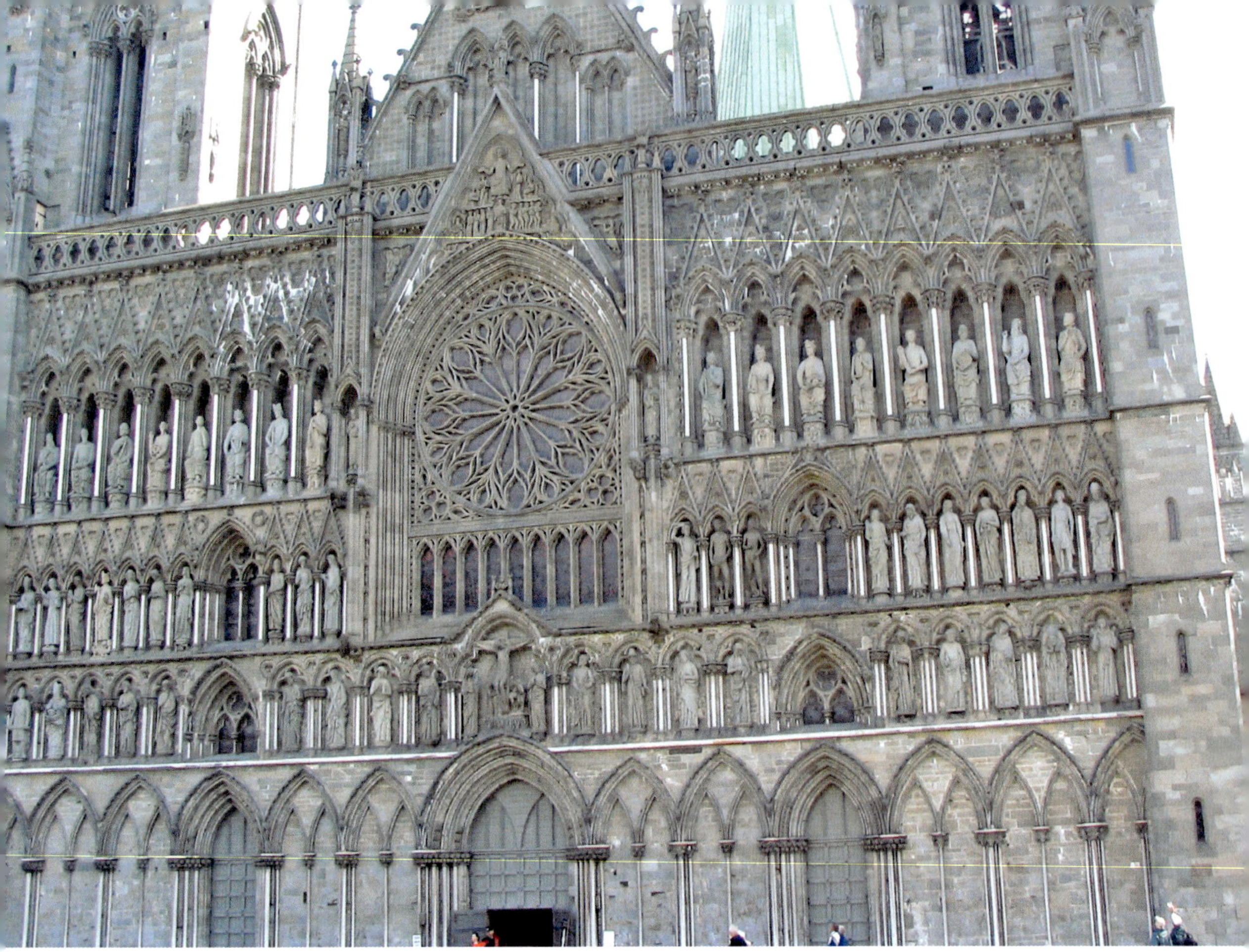

14th July 2006

I drove to Lillehammer, 366 km from Trondheim. Again the journey took time, because most of the road was only a conventional two lane road and was clogged with camper vans. The traffic moved very slowly.

The scenery was much more farmland from just north of Trondheim right the way through to Lillehammer.

Above:
The front of Trondheim Cathedral.

Opposite:
A statue of a ski-jumper in Lillehammer.

Left:
Looking down from the ski jump to the town of Lillehammer.

15th July 2006

Opposite top:
The Circle of Life in Vigeland, Oslo.

Opposite bottom:
The Rathaus, or Town Hall, in Oslo.

I carried on to Oslo, 168 km from Lillehammer and luckily found my way direct to the hotel, arriving by 10.00am.

I wandered around Oslo to the Royal Palace, to the Harbour and then walked out to Vigeland Sculpture Park, which was looking very beautiful with a lot of flowers, as well as the fairly erotic sculptures.

From there I saw the Homenkollen Ski Jump and decided to walk on to see it. The walk took 90 minutes, but was pleasant, as it was a warm day. The view from the top was impressive. A stroll around the museum was interesting, as it showed how ski jumping has improved from 21.5 meters in 1890 to 132.5 meters in the year 2000. The walk back took 2 hours.

Below:
The Royal Palace Oslo.

16th July 2006

I took a ferry across to Bygdøy and visited the Kon Tiki Museum, The Fram Museum and the Viking Museum, which really reflects Norway's reliance on the sea. The museums were all well laid out.

On the way back met a man called Barney, from the Bronx in New York, who had been a diamond dealer and had a beer with him. After I lunch walked around the City.

Opposite top:
The Fram that took Amundsen to Antarctic in the early 1920s.

Left:
Kon-tiki, the balsa wood boat that sailed across the Pacific in 1947.

Opposite bottom:
Viking burial ship built in the 11th Century.

Chapter 9

Sweden

17th July 2006

Today I left Norway for Sweden and drove to Gothenborg. I walked around the City and then contacted Volvo's headquarters, but they were not interested in my journey or problems with the shock absorber. They had started, on that very day, their summer holidays.

The PR Department were totally disinterested, but Customer Services at least tried to be helpful by putting me in touch with one of their agents, so I could get new tyres. Once again, amazingly they did not have any tyre stocks, so decided to wait until I arrived back in the UK before buying new tyres.

Below: A Square Rigger in Gothenburg, Sweden.

18th July 2006

From Gotheburg, I drove to Malmö 276 km away. Malmö is a tourist town, attractive and people were helpful.

I stayed the night at the Quality Hotel.

Right:
Malmö's Rådhus, or Town Hall.

Right:
Two old sailing boats in Malmö harbour.

Chapter 10

Denmark

19th July 2006

After my brief stay in Sweden, I drove the 40 km to Copenhagen. It was a short drive across the 19 km Øresund Bridge and tunnel, which joins Sweden to Denmark.

Copenhagen is a very beautiful City and a wonderful place to stroll through on a sunny day. I went on a canal boat trip, which also took me out in to the harbour to see the famous Little Mermaid, which was surrounded by tourists.

I walked to the Royal Palace and the Marble Church, which is adjacent to the Royal Palace. The Marble Church has the largest dome in Europe and is beautifully painted and very peaceful. At 3.00pm there is a tour up to the top of the dome that I went on. The view from the top was wonderful, looking out over the City.

I continued walking around until I had dinner by one of the canals.

Opposite top:
Wooden light house ship built in 1809 in Copenhagen.

Opposite bottom:
Looking down from the Dome of the Marble Church, Copenhagen.

Below:
Standing by the famous Little Mermaid in Copenhagen.

Above:
St. Albans Church in Copenhagen, close to the statue of the Little Mermaid.

20th July 2006

Leaving Copenhagen, I drove to Aarbenraa in southern Denmark, across two bridges, so that I am now properly on the mainland of Europe, as Copenhagen and Odesse are on islands.

It was a quiet day and in the evening it rained lightly.

Chapter 11

Germany

21st July 2006

Another border crossing, this time into Germany and on to the city of Lübeck, which is a very beautiful city, located on an island

I managed to find a room at the Scandic Hotel, from where I walked all the streets, exploring the city.

Below:
The Rathaus and Market in Lübeck.

22nd July 2006

The next morning I drove the short distance to Hamburg. I was not able to find a room anywhere in the city and was told that the nearest hotel might be 100 km away, as Hamburg had a major music festival on.

So, I decided to drive on to Hanover, which I recall in 1966 was a small attractive city. It certainly has some lovely buildings, but within 100 meters of the centre there is a rough down-market area, which was full of Hells Angels, a minimum of 500 bikes, whose riders were all drinking beer and enjoying a street market.

Eventually I found another large square by the Opera House. Here there was a wine festival taking place and so I enjoyed a couple of glasses. I decided not to stay on in Hanover for the Sunday.

Below:
The New Town Hall in Hanover.

Chapter 12

Belgium

23rd & 24th July 2006

Opposite:
Brussels Town Hall in the Grand Place.

Below:
Parliament Buildings for the European Community seen from the Place du Luxembourg in Brussels.

I was going to drive to Düsseldorf, but decided to go on to Brussels and have two days there.

I stayed in a nice hotel, just outside the Ring Road, but within 15 minutes walk of the centre. Again, very lovely old buildings, many dating back to the 1600s.

25th July 2006

Opposite:
The spire of the Church of Our Lady, Bruges.

Below:
The view of a canal in Bruges.

I made the short journey from Brussels to the mediaeval city of Bruges in western Belgium. Bruges is a charming and beautiful place, with many wonderful buildings and canals to admire.

Chapter 13

France

26th July 2006

Opposite:
The car on the Eurotunnel train, just before leaving Calais for Folkstone and on to home.

From Bruges, I drove to Calais and ended up in St. Omer, about 30 km south of Calais, before crossing back to the UK.

I visited the German V1 launch pad at La Coupole, an interesting site to see, as they could launch up to 15 flying bombs a day. As a small boy I can remember hearing the droning noise of the engine and should that sound stop you knew the bomb was about to come down and blow-up. We were told to immediately take cover or lie down flat on the ground.

27th July 2006

I spent the day visiting Dunkirk and the surrounding area, having been told that a homecoming reception and party had been organised for tomorrow, meaning I needed to delay my Channel crossing by 24 hours!

Below:
A German V1 flying bomb on its launch platform at La Coupole near St. Omer.

XC 90

Chapter 14

The United Kingdom

Above:
From left to right - Judy Reynolds (SightSavers International), the author, Rebecca Muston and Natalie Dendy (Orbis UK).

28th July 2006

The final stretch of this 18,000 mile journey across Asia and Europe was, naturally, one of the simplest, being a 60 mile run up the M20 motorway to my home in Kent.

Upon arrival, I discovered that there was a welcoming committee of family, friends, representatives of SightSavers and Orbis UK, a newspaper journalist, as well as an ITV Meridian News film crew - all of which had been arranged as a surprise by my son, Christopher.

After brief hellos to my family and friends, I was interviewed by the media about the trip. I then spent some time talking about the journey with Judy Reynolds of SightSavers and Rebecca Muston and Natalie Dendy of Orbis UK, before settling down and enjoying the homecoming party.

Conclusion

The trip lasted 100 days from my leaving Dubai, or 92 days on the road. The trip far exceeded my wildest dreams and, amazingly, through the great generosity of friends and acquaintances, realised donations over £175,000.00 for Sightavers and Orbis.

Three days after my return I received a letter from Orbis in China explaining how the £23,000.00 that was raised in the country had been spent, which brought a tear to my eye, as it showed how a relative small amount of money could do so much good, if wisely spent. Six doctors were trained to become eye surgeons, two nurses to be paediatric nurses and 20 women to become eye care visitors. They purchased 12 pieces of sophisticated machinery for eye operations, bought eye test kits and paid for the transportation for 40,000 eye inspections, as well as opening a second eye clinic in the Pingqing district near Chongqing, where a third of the population have eye problems.

Would I undertake a trip like that again? The answer is Yes, provided that the planning was undertaken thoroughly and the various potential risks were calculated before the start, especially when one is travelling on one's own.

What Were The Risks?

Would the car breakdown? Could I buy fuel as required? The car behaved beautifully. I carried two spare wheels plus the basic spares of light bulbs, oil, fan belt and two 20 litre petrol cans. Other than for the bent shock absorber there was no breakdown. Petrol was available everywhere and I disciplined myself to fill up whenever I came across a petrol station, although the octane rating of the petrol did drop to 91 octane for a period and was often 93 octane. However, that appeared not to affect the efficiency of the car.

Volvo at this time did not have any agency or dealership east of Moscow, along the route that I was travelling. I was very disappointed that they would not contribute to the charities, especially as I gave them a CD of the car in places were Volvo had probably not been before.

The fear of high-jacking was a definite possibility in Kazakhstan and Russia and it was for this reason I decided to buy a Ruby Red car, as this would stand out, whereas a silver or white car, which is the norm in thos countries, would not.

I had also not anticipated the role of the police in Kazakhstan, who stopped me on a pretext of speeding to extract bribery money, tried for $1,500 and settled for $200.

The condition of the roads, I realised, was a problem in China, Kazakhstan and Russia. It was only after the trip that I discovered the road running from Kangding towards Lhasa is recognised as the world's third most dangerous road, but that due to the major infrastructure projects being undertaken, it would improved relatively soon.

Kazakhstan's main highway was in places only a sand track, but again improvements were being made.

In Russia the situation is different as the roads are tarmacadam, but only wide enough for two-way traffic. These roads are often rutted due to the large number of heavy goods vehicles.

Food

I decided that I would never eat in a hotel, as so often the food is re-heated, so I took the decision to only eat at cafés where the locals ate. This achieved two ends:

1. I experienced all the local varieties of food which on the whole was most interesting.
2. It allowed me to make conversation with the locals and thus find out more about their way of life and it was having the guides that produced some wonderful moments.

Due to this decision, I never had an upset stomach other than on one occasion. Again any water drunk came from a bottle that I had broken the seal on.

A few weeks after I arrived home I was granted the great honour of meeting Her Royal Highness Princess Alexandra, The Honourable Lady Ogilvy KG GCVO, the President of SightSavers, at Buckingham Palace. Princess Alexandra was very interested to hear about my trip first hand, having been kept up-to-date about the journey, whilst I

Below:
At Buckingham Palace at the invitation of H.R.H. Princess Alexandra.

was on the road.

In September 2006, I flew back to Dubai to return my car's number plate and to reclaim my $10,000 deposit, which all went very smoothly.

Luckily, whilst I was there, the Orbis Flying Eye Hospital landed for a publicity visit and Natalie of Orbis invited me to take a group of friends around the aircraft, which I duly did. Afterwards we went to the Hilton Hotel in Deira where my great friend, Rudi Jaegersbacher, President of Hilton Middle East, laid on a reception and I was allowed to invite the Orbis staff from the aeroplane. We had a great evening. One of the Orbis staff was a nurse, Ann-Marie Ablett, who has given three weeks of her holidays, every year, for 10 years to the Orbis Flying Eye Hospital, despite being a mother.

Whilst visiting my son Simon, his wife and new daughter Chloe, in India where he was working forthree years, I took the opportunity on the 12th October 2012 to visit the Dr. Shroff Eye Hospital in Delhi, one of the first partnerships that Orbis had in India. I was most impressed by the dedication of the doctors and staff at the hospital and how they desired continued support from Orbis, to ensure their quality standards met those set by Orbis.

The Orbis Country Director Dr. Rahul Ali confirmed to me that Orbis now has 30 partner hospitals around India, as well as five in Nepal, which delighted me. Therefore, all the countries with whom I have been involved during my working life now have an Orbis or SightSavers presence.

This book is dedicated to all the doctors, anaesthetists, and nurses, who volunteer to work with Orbis, or who give up their time for free, to undertake operations to give sight back or prevent deterioration of the sight of children, on board the Flying Eye Hospital. Whilst the operations are being performed in the back of the aeroplane, doctors and anaesthetists from the partner hospitals are watching the operations via television screens, to learn how to perform such intricate operations. The operating theatre has 17 cameras filming, so that everything can be watched and talked through by the operating surgeon.

In their spare time these volunteers visit the local partner hospitals again to watch and where necessary advise the local doctors, anaesthetists, nurses go about their work and the medical volunteers, who go out in to the countryside to identify children, who need assistance. At the

Above:
Orbis's Flying Eye Hospital in Dubai in September 2006.

same time, where feasible, they teach improved hygienic standards.

Donations

Should you wish to donate to either Orbis or SightSavers International, please look at their websites and donate, as a small amount of money goes a long way to changing the lives of those who are needlessly blind, or have impaired vision that prevents them from taking part in an active life.

The websites are:-
www.orbis.org.uk
www.sightsavers.org

The moral of the journey "18,000km to Save Sight" is that whatever the problems that lie in your way, there is always a route that can be taken and people who will help you, provided you are determined, persevere and are polite.

This was certainly true in my case. It is all too easy to give up, but you will be left with your dreams unfilled. For the children that are blind, throughout the world, there should always be hope, as there are all those generous doctors, anaesthetists and nurses who give their time to save sight with charities such as Orbis and SightSavers.

All of the profits from the sale of this book will be donated equally between SightSavers International and Orbis UK.

Appendix 1

President Hu Jintao Letters

His Excellency Mr Hu Jintao,
General Secretary,
Central Committee of the Communist Party of China,
C/o The Consulate General of Dubai
United Arab Emirates

23rd February 2005.

Your Excellency

I hope that I am not wasting your time but would like to seek your permission to undertake a trip that I have had in my thoughts for many years and that is to drive through China.

Sir, I have had the pleasure to visit China twice within the last fifteen months for business purposes and am very impressed with your country, its current developments and the hospitality of your fellow countrymen. I work for the Future Pipe Group and am responsible, as one of my functions, for the purchase of Fiberglass for our pipe manufacturing factories spread throughout the Middle East, Europe and the USA and in 2004 have purchased 30,000 Metric Tons from China the majority of which has come from the Jushi Group in Tongxiang. I believe the President Mr Zhang Yuqiang would vouch for me.

I am planning to retire in July as I have reached the young age of 66 and would like to finish my main career by undertaking a journey that few others, if any, have ever had the opportunity to experience by driving to the United Kingdom by first flying from Dubai to Shanghai where I would arrange to collect a new vehicle, but only if you would be gracious enough to grant me your permission, to drive from Shanghai through Chongqing, Chengdu, Llasa and cross out to Kyrgyzstan from Kashi. From there I propose to drive through Kazakhstan, Russia, Finland over the Arctic Circle and finally down the length of Norway to the UK, a distance that I estimate to be some 10,500 miles. I plan to make the journey by myself as my wife died three years ago. If you would require me to be accompanied by a Chinese guide, provided they could speak English as I only have a very few words of Chinese, I would have no problem.

This would not be the first such journey as I had an opportunity in 1968 when I completed an assignment in Kenya and on that occasion I drove from Karachi, Pakistan, over the Khyber Pass through Afghanistan, Iran, Georgia, Russia, Finland and Norway but that route is now not possible to repeat.

My full name is Nicholas Peter Archibald WHITE, my address in England is 'The Stables, Canon Lane, Wateringbury, Nr Maidstone, Kent ME18 5PQ. I will be applying within two weeks for a new Business Visa to visit the Jushi Group on the 15th April 2005.

Would you please inform me through your staff the procedure that I should follow if you are able to approve my request to drive across China. Attached is the route that I would suggest and propose to travel.

Sir, I seek your support for me to enter in to retirement having achieved this long-term ambition. Could you please advise me of your decision at the earliest opportunity so that I can continue with my plans to obtain approval for the other countries.

Yours sincerely

Sir Nicholas White
Vice President - Administration

Proposed Journey of
Nicholas Peter Archibald White
May – July 2006.

Shanghai
Tongxiang
Hangzhou
Jiujiang
Wuhan
Chongqing
Chengdu
Ya'an
Matkam
Rawu
Gyimda
Llasa
Llase
Moincer
Wujiang
Mazar
Kashi
Cross to Kyrgyzstan
At-Bashy
Kara Balta to Kazakhstan
Shymkent
Aral'sk
Uralsk to Russia
Kuznetsk
Ryuzan
Moscow
St Petersburg to Finland
Lahti
Oulu
Ivalo to Norway
Kistand
Narvik
Trondheim
Oslo on to United Kingdom

23.02.2005.

中华人民共和国国家旅游局
National Tourism Administration of the People's Republic of China
No. 9A Jian Guo Men Nei Ave., Beijing 100740, China
Tel: 0086 - 10 - 65201114 Fax: 0086 - 10 - 65122096

The Stables, Canon Lane
Wateringbury, Nr Maidstone
Kent ME18 5PQ
Great Britain

April 11, 2005

ATT: Letter to request a driving tour around China on February 23, 2005

Dear Sir Nicolas White:

Your letter to Mr. Hu Jintao, General Secretary of Central Committee of the Communist Party of China was received with pleasure. We highly appreciate your cordiality and special feeling towards China and its people. So you are welcome to travel by driving your car across China, a great and magnificent country.

According to our policy, foreigners need to apply for an approval to drive their own vehicle across China. Herein we would like to assist you in providing the following information:

First you need to select a capable travel service company to make land operation on your behalf. We may recommend some to you if you have such a request. Then you are required to submit through the travel service company three month in advance the latter documents to China National Tourism Administration for approval, such as your personal data, travel plan (including entry and exit port, time, routes and itinerary, major cities and towns to stay and activities to be conducted) and information of your vehicle.

Once the approval is granted, you may make your driving tour according to the approved itinerary, time and program with your travel guide designated by the travel service company.

We wish you a wonderful and successful journey with beautiful impression in China.

Should you have any more questions, you may feel free to contact Mr. Li Mingxing at 0086-10-65201602 (Fax Number: 0086-10-65201655). He may answer the phone in English.

Yours sincerely,

Mrs. Li Yaying
Deputy Director General
Marketing and Communications Department
China National Tourism Administration

尼古拉斯：38年前曾开车穿越六国

东方早报记者　姚秋韵　　　2006-4-26 1:08:22

飞抵上海之后，尼古拉斯除了忙于办证件，偶尔也会忙里偷闲步行到外滩看看夕阳下的浦江。满头银发，鬓角齐整，衣衫雅致，倾听时温和沉静，交谈时会周到地放慢语速。旁人总是很难将如此一位标准的英国绅士与计划驾车横跨亚欧大陆的“疯狂”举动联系在一起。面对他人的困惑神情，他说：“我在进行前所未有的举动。”

早报：旅行线路是自己设计的吗？为什么选择中国作为旅行的起点？

尼古拉斯：我买回了一套世界地图集，便开始在地图上标注国家与城市。选择中国是因为西藏，那里是我梦寐以求的地方。我想只有通过这次旅行，我才能对中国，对东方有清楚的认识。

早报：在旅行之前有没有接受全面的身体检查？行李中准备了哪些药品？

尼古拉斯：当然有，医生说我很健康。我坚持去健身房运动，两年前我还曾经去过尼泊尔高原，没有任何不适应。我准备了一些常备药品，其中包括治疗感冒、头晕，降低血液黏度的药品，以及备不时之需的氧气。

早报：你以前有过类似的长途跋涉吗？

尼古拉斯：1968年，当我结束在肯尼亚和坦桑尼亚四年的海外任职，我没有选择乘飞机离开，而是从卡拉奇出发，开车穿越了巴基斯坦、阿富汗、伊朗、前苏联、芬兰和挪威六国，最后回到英伦。这次的行程从莫斯科开始大致与1968年的吻合。

早报：有没有想过会半途而废？

尼古拉斯：从来没有，我相信一定能完成。

早报：整个行程需要花费多少钱？全部自费吗？

尼古拉斯：预计大约要用去4万美元（约合34万元人民币），都由我自己承担。尽管如此，我依然觉得这将是一次既有趣又有意义的旅行，沿途每一个国家的风土人情，历史文化宗教特色，都将被记录并发布在我的个人网站上。

计划经过的12个国家：

中国、哈萨克斯坦、乌兹别克斯坦、俄罗斯、芬兰、挪威、瑞典、丹麦、德国、荷兰、比利时、英国集团在中国境内的原料供应商，希望他们能够为慈善事业献出爱心。而奥比斯代表也表示，凡是在与奥比斯建立了合作关系的中国城市中，奥比斯会尽可能地为尼古拉斯提供帮助。

尼古拉斯同时通过东方早报向社会宣布，任何形式的捐助都不会与他本人发生接触，他所做的只是奔走相告，如果想要为失明者提供帮助，可以直接联系ORBIS 中国上海办事处，通过登录 ORBIS 的中国网站或者尼古拉斯的个人网站（http://www.18000kmtosavesight.org）了解其他详细情况。

[大都会] 上海启程 英国绅士驾车跨亚欧

东方早报记者　姚秋韵　06-4-26 1:14:24

昨天下午，67 岁的英国人尼古拉斯·怀特在上海的车辆交通管理部门顺利通过考核，拿到了中国境内的临时驾照，一旦他的红色沃尔沃 SUV 运抵中国，他就将开始自己的横跨亚欧的宏大之旅。按照怀特的计划，他将穿越中国、哈萨克斯坦、乌兹别克斯坦、俄罗斯、芬兰、挪威、瑞典、丹麦、德国、荷兰、比利时，终点是英国，全程 18000 公里。

上海翻译会陪到宜川

尼古拉斯 • 怀特原来是阿联酋 FuturePipe 集团的副总裁。2004 年末，面临退休的他计划以驾车跨国旅行的方式回到自己的国家。

2005 年 2 月，尼古拉斯提笔给中国政府写信，详细陈述了自己的意图并希望获得政府的批准。很快，国家旅游总局便以书信的形式给了他回复，不仅对于他的计划和寻求翻译帮助的设想表示同意，并委托国旅集团来配合他完成中国的行程。

经过近一年的准备，2006 年 4 月 20 日，尼古拉斯从迪拜飞抵上海，边办理在中国境内必需的相关手续，边等待自己的心爱座驾运抵上海随时准备开始行程。国旅集团新上海国际旅行社的有关负责人表示，尼古拉斯在中国期间大致会有 5 到 6 个段陪翻译，其中上海国旅的翻译会陪同他到达宜川，与当地国旅的段陪完成交接。而一旦从新疆霍尔果斯边境办理完出境手续，接下来的行程将全部由尼古拉斯独自完成。

尼古拉斯在中国境内将停留的城市包括杭州、景德镇、武汉、宜川、重庆、成都、拉萨等，在穿越青藏高原，抵达拉萨之后，他将从敦煌开始进入悠远的丝绸之路。

为贫苦失明者筹款

原本只是单纯的退休旅行，但在 2005 年 11 月的某一天，当尼古拉斯收看了 BBC 关于慈善组织救治失明者的纪录片后，他决定在旅行计划中加入为慈善事业募捐的部分。

2005 年圣诞节期间，尼古拉斯在英国与慈善治盲机构“OR－BIS”和“SIGHTSAVERS”代表见面并表达了要尽力为这些组织募集资金的想法。他希望募得善款可以用于在过去 48 年间他所工作过的国家，包括：尼泊尔、肯尼亚、坦桑尼亚、印度、巴基斯坦、阿联酋和中国。

通过早报呼吁募捐

昨天，奥比斯（ORBIS）中国区代表与尼古拉斯取得了联系，双方详谈了关于在中国境内的合作事宜。尼古拉斯说，他将会在旅行中拜访所有 FuturePipe

Appendix 2

The Planned Route

18,000 KM TO SAVE SIGHT

SHANGHAI TO LONDON VIA THE NORTH CAPE

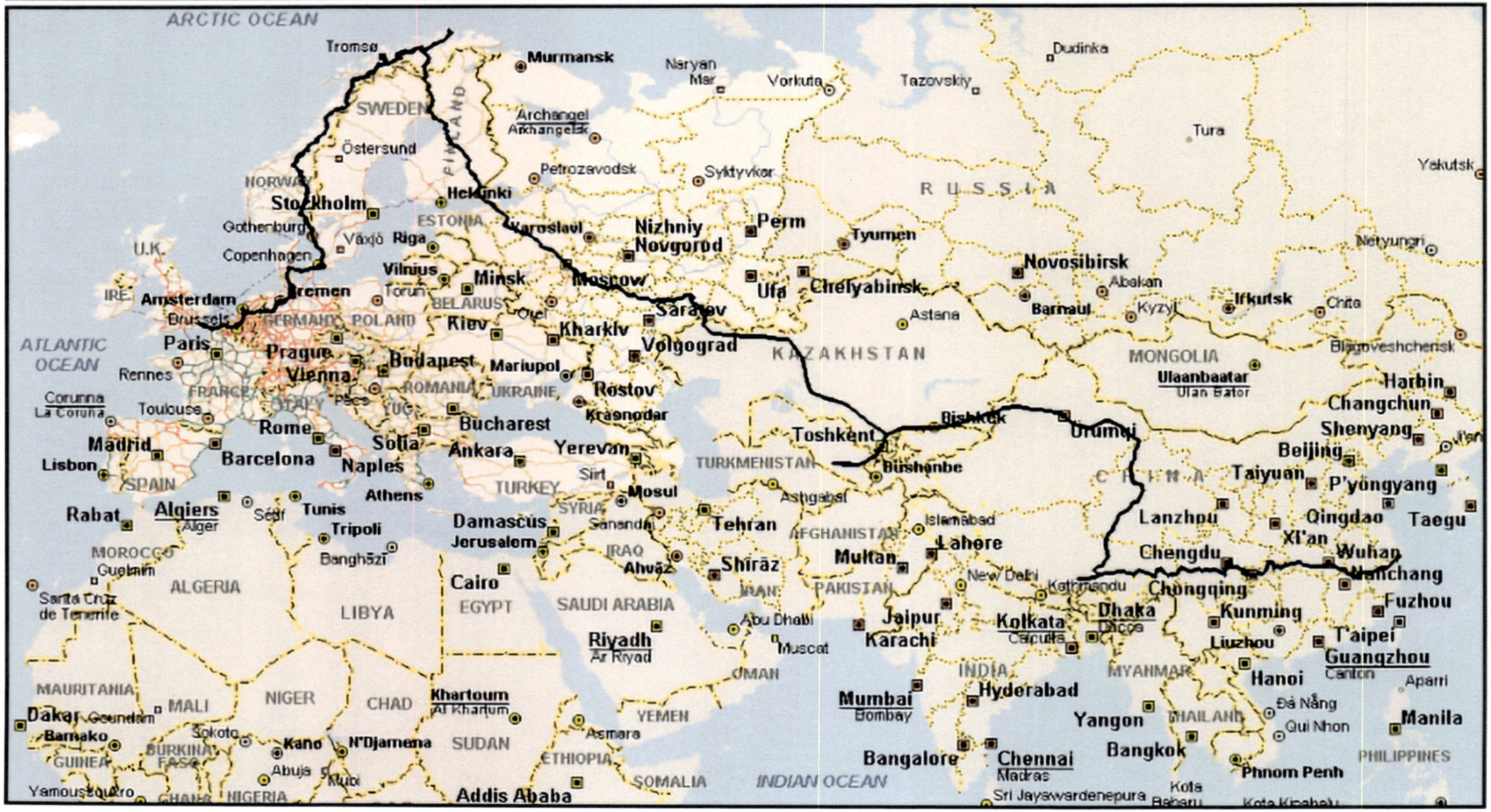

The Route To Be Followed

20 April	Fly to Shanghai
21 – 24 April	Stay in Shanghai
25 April	Start Journey drive to Hangzhou, famous for Silk
26 April	Drive Jingdezhen, famous porcelain onto Jiujiang
27 April	Drive Wuhan
28 April	Drive Yichang and visit Three Gorges Dam
29 April	In Yichang
30 April	Drive to Enshi (by the Yangtze River)
1 May	Drive to Wanxian (by the Yangtze)
2 May	Drive to Chongqing
3 May	Stay Chongquin
4 May	Drive to Dazu, Visit the Dazu Grotto and drive to Chengdu
5 May	Stay Chengdu, visit Panda Sanctuary and Sanxingdui
6 May	Drive to Leshan to visit the Great Buddha
7 May	Drive to Ya'an and go on to Kangding
8 May	Drive to Litang
9 May	Drive to Batang
10 May	Drive to Markham
11 May	Drive to Zuogong (Wangda) and to Basu (Bama)
12 May	Drive to Rawu and to Bomi (Zhamu)
13 May	Drive to Nyinchi
14 May	Stay in Nyinchi
15 May	Drive to Lhasa
16 May	Stay in Lhasa
17 May	Stay in Lhasa
18 May	Drive to Shigartze
19 May	Drive to Lhasa
20 May	Drive to Naqu
21 May	Drive to Tanggula Mountain (5,700 meters)
22 May	Drive to Golmut
23 May	Drive to Dunhuang
24 May	Stay in Dunhuang, visit famous Grottoes
26 May	Drive to Hami
27 May	Drive to Turpan (second lowest spot on Earth)

28 May	Stay Turpan
29 May	Drive to Kuitin
30 May	Drive to Yining
31 May	Stay Yining
1 June	Drive to Holgus
2 June	Cross to Almaty in Kazakhstan
3 June	Stay Almaty
4 June	Stay Almaty
05 June	Drive to Korday
06 June	Drive to Taraz
07 June	Drive to Tashkent, Uzbekistan
08 June	Drive to Samarakand
09 June	Stay Samarakand
10 June	Drive to Buchara
11 June	Stay Bukhara
12 June	Drive to Yurt Camp Aidarkul Lake
13 June	Drive to Tashkent
14 June	Drive Tashkent to Shymkent in Kazakhstan
15 June	Drive to Zhargaqorghau
16 June	Drive to Kyzylorda
17 June	Drive to Aral'sk
18/19 June	Aral'sk Sea
20 June	Drive to Irgiz
21 June	Drive to Karabutak
22 June	Drive to Aktyubinsk
23 June	Drive to Zhympity
24 June	Drive to Ural'sk
25 June	Cross to the Federation of Russia and to Samara
26 June	Drive to Syzran
27 June	Drive to Ulyanovsk
28 June	Drive to Kazan via Tsivil'sk
29 June	Kazan
30 June	Kazan
1 July	Drive to Nizlniy Novgorod via Tsivil'sk
2 July	Drive Vladimir
3 July	Drive Moscow

4 July	Stay Moscow
5 July	Stay Moscow
6 July	Drive Visniy – Volocheck
7 July	Drive St Petersburg
8 July	Stay St Petersburg
9 July	Stay St Petersburg
10 July	Drive via Vyborg to Hamina in Finland
11 July	Drive to Helsinki
12 July	Stay in Helsinki
13 July	Drive to Lahti
14 July	Drive to Jyvaskyla
15 July	Drive to Oulu
16 July	Drive to Rovaniemi
17 July	Drive to Ivalo
18 July	Drive to Karigasmeni and on to Karasjok, in Norway
19 July	Drive to Lakselv and Kistand
20 July	Drive to Nordcapp
21 July	Drive to Skaisdi
22 July	Drive to Strorslett
23 July	Drive to Nordkjosbotn
24 July	Drive to Narvik
25 July	Stay in Narvik
26 July	Drive to Fauske
27 July	Drive to Mosjoen
28 July	Drive to Steenkjor
29 July	Drive to Trondheim
30 July	Stay Trondheim
31 July	Drive to Dombas
1 August	Drive to Lillehammer
2 August	Drive to Oslo
3 August	Stay Oslo
4 August	Drive to Gothenborg in Sweden
5 August	Stay Gothenburg
6 August	Drive to Halmstad
7 August	Drive to Malmo
8 August	Drive to Copenhagen in Denmark

9 August	Stay in Copenhagen
10 August	Drive to Kolding
11 August	Drive to Schleswig in Germany
12 August	Drive to Hamburg
13 August	Drive to Cloppenburg
14 August	Drive to Hengelo in Holland
15 August	Drive to Eindhoven
16 August	Drive to Brussels in Belgium
17 August	Drive to Brugge
18 August	Drive to Channel Tunnel France and UK

Total 121 Days from 20 April to 18 August.

Nicholas White
22nd March 2006.

Summary of The Second Week of Driving In China

This week has been an experience but one which I have thoroughly enjoyed although in places has been a bit hairy.

The car has performed excellently even at 5008 meters the highest pass so far crossed. The roads in many areas have been dirt stony road with earth spread to smoothen out the surface, the only problem with this is that when it is dry which has been every day except for the last the earth throws up a powder dust which permeates through the AC and makes following another vehicle difficult especially if you are tying to overtake an over laden lorry or one of the innumerable buses. When the road is wet as it was yesterday the powder dirt becomes slippery.

In certain places the road has been diabolical and really was not able to be called a highway although it is the main road from Shanghai to Lhasa and Kathmandu. In places the road was just wide enough for a lorry and one place where a new road is being constructed you ran along a track that had enormous potholes and water flowing across the road for 20 km. In another yesterday the road was slippery, came to the top of a rise and could not see what was over the other side and hoped for the best as on the left there was an unguarded drop of 300 feet or so, luckily there was nothing coming in the opposite direction and I would not liked to have tried reversing.

- In the first week the car drove 3,044 km and used 389 litres of fuel = averaged 7.825 km per litre (18.41 mpg).
- In the second week which was chiefly 80% non made-up road the distance covered was 2,089 km using 272 litres of fuel = an average of 7.68 km per litre (18.06 mpg).

Summary of The 3rd and 4th Weeks of Driving In China

I have now nearly crossed China and Tibet, have experience the height of 5,231 meters above sea level and 154 meters below sea level near Turpan. The roads from Lhasa in Tibet to Turpan in Xinjiang Province have generally been very good especially in Xinjiang.

The off-road work has been when I have been sight-seeing, such as the Forest that did not exist and going down to the Salt Lake in the Depression in Turpan, which were pretty atrocious. The Volvo has performed brilliantly and I hope that remains the case.

The weather that I have experienced as ranged from -5°C with snow to 46°C hot and sunny. To date, I have only had two days of wet/snow weather, otherwise every day has been sunny.

Driving standards have been generally good, except for the taxis, three-wheeler Tuk-tuk vehicles and the tractors that never appear to look before turning. Cyclist are cyclists the world over!

The last 2½ weeks of driving has produced a better fuel consumption, as there have been few mountains to wind through, with an average speed of about 100 kph.

- 12th - 23rd May drove 3,100 km and consumed 319.81 litres = an average of 9.6932 km per litre (22.8 mpg).
- 25th - 30th May drove 2,370 km and consumed 286.03 litres = an average of 8.2858 km per litre (19.49 mpg).

Total distance driven to Yining, including sight-seeing, 10,603 km and used 1,267 litres of fuel = 8.368 km per litre (19.68 mpg).

I estimate that all the zigzagging in the mountains probable cost me 700 - 1,000 km, which I had not accounted for. The so-called straight route has been 9,357 km with the sight-seeing adding some 1,246 km.

Highway Tolls cost RMB 1,304 (US$ 163). There were no Tolls in Tibet, but they started again from Golmud to Yining.

Appendix 3

The Appeal Letter

Sir Nicholas White, Bt.
c/o Future Pipe Industries LLC
PO Box 1371
Dubai, UAE

Dear Sir or Madam,

"18,000 km to Save Sight"

An Invitation to Help Combat Needless Blindness

In April I will be undertaking an unusual journey which will enable me to realize the long held ambitions to visit Tibet and raise a £1 million for charity.

My aim is to raise funds for the hugely worthwhile cause of eliminating preventable blindness in the world by supporting the global initiative, VISION 2020: The Right to Sight. There are 37 million people who are blind in the world today and the majority of them live in the poorer nations of Africa, the Indian sub-continent and Asia. A staggering 75% of this blindness is preventable or curable - for example, cataract is the world's leading cause of blindness and an estimated 17 million people are blind as a result of the condition. More shockingly, cataract sufferers can be given back their sight through a simple operation that can cost as little as £17.00.

In 1999 the World Health Organization and the International Agency for the Prevention of Blindness established VISION 2020, a global initiative involving a number of non government organisations concerned with eye care. The initiative aims to eliminate avoidable blindness by the year 2020 and prevent 100 million people from going blind.
Having obtained the initial approval for my trip from the Governments concerned, I am seeking financial support to act as an incentive and to give my journey a real objective, not only for me personally but also for the VISION 2020 initiative.

My aim is to raise over £1 million, to help thousands of individuals receive the eye care treatment or services they so desperately need, while at the same time helping to reduce the personal and financial burden on their families and communities as a whole. The United Arab Emirates and the G.C.C. rely heavily upon employees from these poorer nations and I am sure we have all heard of the numerous hardship cases that so many of our employees and relations suffer in their home countries.

I am writing to ask if you will be generous in pledging money to the Nicholas White Eye Care Fund "18,000 km to Save Sight" by sending your generous pledges to either Sight Savers International or Orbis direct and referring to "18,000 km to Save Sight".

By writing your cheque directly to one of these two charities you can be assured that every penny of the money donated will end up by being spent on a worthwhile cause as I have agreed with them how the money is to be used in the countries that I wish to be assisted by these two VISION 2020's founding member organizations, Sight Savers International and ORBIS, for use through their local partnerships to provide eye care in Nepal, Kenya, Tanzania, India, Pakistan, UAE and China. These are all countries with which I have been involved during my working life.

If you require any further information concerning the Charities, please feel free to contact Judy Reynolds at Sight Savers International on 0044 1444 446667 or Rebecca Muston of Orbis on 0044 207 6087263.

As His Highness Sheikh Mohamed Bin Rashid Al Maktoum, UAE Vice President, Prime Minister and Ruler of Dubai was reported to have said at the opening of the DIFC "Most people talk – we do things. They plan – we achieve. They hesitate – we move ahead. We are a living proof that when human beings have the courage and commitment to transform a dream into reality there is nothing that can stop them. Dubai is a living example of that". This is what I am trying to achieve and so thank you in advance for your generosity in helping to support this most worthwhile cause. With your support we can transform the lives of thousands of individuals suffering from needless blindness so that they can live more independently.

You may be interested to watch my journey's progress by viewing my interactive website www.18000kmtosavesight.org that will be updated regularly.

With gratitude and warm regards,

Yours sincerely,

Nicholas White

Sir Nicholas White

Details for donations direct to the Charities

Orbis UK

Charity registration No. 1061352

Bank details

Account Name	**Orbis**
Sort Code	**40-05-33**
Account Number	**81185942**
Or International Account	**GB34MIDL40053381185942 (for non UK Donors)**
Branch Identifier	**MIDLGB2105J**

Please mention reference "18000 km to Save Sight"

Address	**Orbis** **4th Floor, Fergusson House** **124 – 128 City Road** **London EC1V 2NJ**
Website	**www.orbis.org.uk**

Sight Savers International

Charity Registration No. 207544

Bank details

Account Name	**Sight Savers HICA**
Sort Code	**40-23-27**
Account Number	**41270095**
International Account No.	**GB69MIDL40232741270095 (for non UK Donors)**

Please mention my Ref 62665251 "18000 km to Save Sight"

Address	**Sight Savers International** **Bolnore Road** **Haywards Heath** **West Sussex RH16 4BX**
Website	**www.sightsavers.org.uk**

sightsavers
INTERNATIONAL

ORBIS
saving sight worldwide

18,000 km to Save Sight

On 24th April 2006, Sir Nicholas White, Bt. will be embarking upon an unusual trip that will fulfil two of his lifelong ambitions: to visit Tibet and to raise over £1 million for charity.

His aim is to raise funds for the hugely worthwhile cause of eliminating preventable blindness in the world by supporting the global initiative, VISION 2020: The Right to Sight.

BLINDNESS

There are 37 million people who are blind in the world today - predominantly in the poorer nations of Africa, the Indian sub-continent and Asia. A staggering 75% of this blindness is preventable or curable. For example, an estimated 17 million people are blind as a result of cateracts - the world's leading cause of blindness. More shockingly, cateract sufferers can be given back their sight by a simple operation costing as little as £17.00.

In 1999 the World Health Organisation and the International Agency for the Prevention of Blindness established VISION 2020, a global initiative involving a number of non-government agencies concerned with eye care. The initiative aims to eliminate avoidable blindness by the year 2020 and prevent 100 million people from going blind.

THE TRIP

Sir Nicholas is undertaking this marathon trip to support the registered charities Sight Savers International and ORBIS.

The trip will commence on 24th April 2006 from Shanghai in China and take him through China, Tibet, Kazakhstan, Uzbekistan, Russia, Finland, Norway, Sweden, Denmark, Germany, Holland, Belgium and France, before arriving home in Kent in mid-August.

Sir Nicholas will be doing the trip fully unsupported and expects to cover just over 18,000km. He believes this will be the longest continuous road trip ever undertaken without the use of additional means of transport, such as ferries!

You will be able to follow his progress and read regular updates from the road on the website below.

DONATIONS

The serious side to the project is to raise substantial funds for the aforementioned charities. All monies received will go directly to projects which will benefit people in Nepal, Kenya, Tanzania, India, Pakistan, UAE and China. These are all countries with which Sir Nicholas has been involved during his working life.

If you do require any further information concerning the Charities, please feel free to contact Judy Reynolds at Sight Savers on 01444 446667 or Rebecca Muston of Orbis on 020 76087263.

You can be assured that any that every penny of the money donated will end up by being spent on a worthwhile cause as Sir Nicholas has agreed with them how the money is to be used.

As His Highness Sheikh Mohamed Bin Rashid Al Maktoum, UAE Vice President, Prime Minister and Ruler of Dubai was reported to have said at the opening of the DIFC "Most people talk - we do things. They plan - we achieve. They hesitate - we move ahead. We are a living proof that when human beings have the courage and commitment to transform a dream into reality there is nothing that can stop them. Dubai is a living example of that".

This is what Sir Nicholas White is trying to achieve and so thank you in advance for your generosity in helping to support this most worthwhile cause.

With your support we can transform lives of thousands of individuals suffering from needless blindness so that they can live more independently.

HOW TO DONATE

Donations can be made directly by bank transfer to the charities, or cheques can be sent to either Sight Savers International or ORBIS at the below addresses. Please always mention the appropriate references given below.

Orbis UK

4th Floor, Fergusson House
124 – 128 City Road
London EC1V 2NJ
Website: www.orbis.org.uk

Charity registration No. 1061352

Bank details

Account Name:	Orbis
Sort Code:	40-05-33
Account Number:	81185942

International Account GB34MIDL40053381185942 (for non UK donors)
Branch Identifier: MIDLGB2105J

Please mention reference "18000 km to Save Sight"

Sight Savers International

Bolnore Road
Haywards Heath
West Sussex RH16 4BX
Website: www.sightsavers.org.uk

Charity Registration No. 207544

Bank Details

Account Name:	Sight Savers HICA
Sort Code:	40-23-27
Account Number:	41270095

International Account No.
GB69MIDL40232741270095 (for non UK donors)

Please mention Ref 62665251 "18000 km to Save Sight"

www.18000kmtosavesight.org

Sight Savers International & ORBIS

An introduction to the organisations supported by the Nicholas White Eye Care Fund "18,000 kms to Save Sight"

The issue

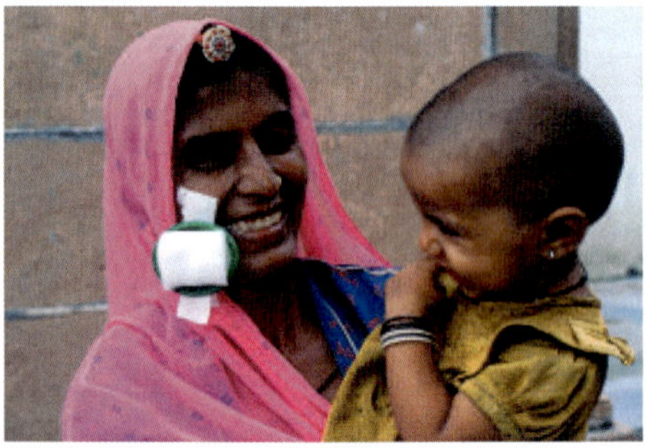

Kanku, from Rajasthan in India, holds her baby, Umarao, after cataract surgery.

Today, there are an estimated 37 million blind people worldwide, with a further 124 million with severe visual impairment. Every five seconds one person in our world goes blind and one child goes blind every minute. 75% of these people are suffering needlessly, as their blindness could be prevented or treated. This avoidable blindness is inextricably linked with poverty: millions go blind for lack of simple treatment and millions stay blind for lack of simple surgery. Yet activities to prevent and treat blindness are amongst the most cost-effective in the world, with sight-restoring cataract surgery costing in some countries as little as £17.

The World Health Organisation estimates that without intervention, the number of people who are blind could increase to 76 million by the year 2020, increasing the social and economic impact on individuals, families and communities in developing countries.

The leading causes of blindness are either preventable or curable and include:

Cataract - The leading cause of blindness with around 17 million blind as a result of this cloudiness of the lens. Affecting both adults and children, it cannot be prevented but is easy and cost effective to cure with a 20 minute operation to replace the lens.

Trachoma - Trachoma is another common cause of blindness and is particularly rife in parts of the developing world. It is caused by an infection spread by flies and cross infection. It can be prevented easily with environmental and personal hygiene or antibiotic treatment. Years of infection leads to **trichiasis**, when the eyelid turns inwards, causing the eyelashes to rub on the surface of the eye which is terribly painful. If the condition is left untreated, it will eventually lead to blindness. Trichiasis can be cured with a simple operation costing on average £5.

River Blindness - Found primarily in Africa, this disease is caused by a parasite which once in the body causes terrible itching and skin problems and on reaching the eye, blindness. It is easily preventable with an annual single dose of Mectizan® donated by Merck & Co.

VISION 2020: The Right to Sight

To combat preventable blindness Sight Savers & ORBIS have joined forces with the World Health Organisation (WHO) and other eye care non governmental organisations (NGO's) to form VISION 2020.

VISION 2020 is a global initiative which aims to eliminate avoidable blindness by the year 2020 working collaboratively with more than 20 international NGO's involved in eye care and prevention and management of blindness.

The good news is that since the start of this new initiative the number of people who are blind has reduced due to the long-term work of VISION 2020. The success in tackling the causes of blindness as well as the important work of improving the statistical information on blindness has led to this reduction.

Evidence of the effectiveness of the VISION 2020 programme can be seen for example in India where the numbers of people who are blind has dropped from 9 to 6.7 million people, a decrease of 25% in 10 years. The global figures for trachoma are also dropping mainly due to the improvement in treatment, water provision, hygiene and sanitation.

About the Organisations:

Sight Savers

For over fifty years Sight Savers has been working with local partners to combat blindness in developing countries and support people who are irreversibly blind through education, training and counselling. During this time, we have helped restore sight to more than five million people and treat over 80 million for potentially blinding conditions. Sight Savers' support reaches the people who need it the most – individuals living in some of the poorest countries in the world. We work with local partners to ensure that services are developed that are appropriate to local needs.

How we work

In recent years, Sight Savers has developed and begun to implement Comprehensive Eye Services (CES) programmes in countries around the world. CES programmes offer an integrated package of services to a specific district or region, including screening and treatment to prevent eye disease, health education and curative surgical eye care, aftercare and training for all levels of ophthalmic personnel. Within these programmes, we will also support services for people who are irreversibly blind, including education for children and community-based rehabilitation for adults. Through comprehensive eye services, staff are trained to recognise all eye conditions and refer them as necessary. This ensures that people receive the most appropriate treatment, irrespective of age, type, severity of visual impairment, and that eye care provision is available long term.

ORBIS
37 million people worldwide are blind, yet 28 million of them have eye conditions that could be treated or prevented.

ORBIS was formed in 1982 as a practical solution to this overwhelming problem. We work in partnership with local health professionals and members of the community to improve the quality of eye care available for people where the need is greatest. A cure is often simple and inexpensive, but in the world's poorest countries even the most basic medical help is often out of reach for those who need it the most.

ORBIS training gives local medical professionals the skills to treat and prevent conditions that cause blindness and to manage local eye care systems. With the help of local community groups, we use education programmes to raise awareness of eye conditions and teach people how to prevent them. A vital part of our work is the support of eye care facilities such as paediatric centres. We make sure that local hospitals and clinics have the medication and technology they need to diagnose and treat conditions and crucially, we train personnel to repair and maintain equipment to ensure that resources are sustainable.

Wherever we work, our focus is to develop the accessibility and quality of eye care through a combination of medical and biomedical training, improved eye care facilities for rural populations and education of the general public.

Twenty-four years later, our highly skilled volunteer medical staff have trained over 100,000 local medical professionals in 83 countries who have gone on to share their new skills with others and give millions of people back their sight and their future.

The Nicholas White Eye Care Fund "18,000 kms to Save Sight"

Sir Nicholas White is requesting sponsorship for his trip to raise funds for Sight Savers and ORBIS, two of VISION 2020's founding members. By supporting Sir Nicholas, you can make a real and lasting difference to the lives of many people in China, UAE, India, Kenya, Nepal, Pakistan & Tanzania who are suffering unnecessarily for want of some simple treatment, training or support.

Details of specific projects that the funds raised from this appeal will support are available on request.

Appendix 4

Press Coverage

BRITAIN in BUSINESS

BRITISH BUSINESS GROUP
DUBAI & NORTHERN EMIRATES

The magazine of the
British Business Group
Dubai & Northern Emirates

It's no pipe dream...

Nick White plans to raise £1 million to battle blindness

Shanghai Daily.com

Briton sets off on charity trip

Yuan Qi
2006-04-25

NICHOLAS White, a 67-year-old Briton, will begin his 18,000-kilometer global charity journey from Shanghai today to collect donations for needy cataract patients in seven countries where he worked during his career.

An engineer by profession, White worked in Nepal, Kenya, Tanzania, India, Pakistan, the United Arab Emirates and China, for a global fiber-glass pipe company.

During this time he found that many poor people suffering from cataract could not afford the operation, although they could easily be cured.

"I have seen thousands of people living in the dark because of cataract," said White. "Just a small operation can help them see light again, but they can't even afford to pay the meager fees."

The average cost of a cataract operation is usually under US$30. However, it's still beyond many patients' reach.

White hopes the money he raises during his around-the-world trip, details of which even he is not sure, can help cataract patients in the seven countries regain their sight.

Since most of these countries are in Asia, White has decided to drive his own Volvo across the continent and then move into former Soviet Union territory. He will start from Shanghai and will traverse most provinces of China, including moving through the Three Gorges area and Xinjiang Uygur Autonomous Region. His last stop in China is Lhasa, capital of Tibet.

"After reaching Lhasa, I will continue my drive to Russia, Uzbekistan and Kazakhstan. According to my plan, the entire distance for the journey will be around 18,000 kilometers," White said, without revealing where his trek will finally end.

The trip is expected to raise about 1 million pounds (US$1.8 million) in charity. Individuals or enterprises are welcome to pitch in. All donations will be under the administration of the Orbis International Foundation.

"My aim is to draw more people's attention to the blind," said White.

The Khaleej Times, Dubai

25th April 2006

Setting out in support of drive against blindness

SIR NICHOLAS WHITE WILL TRAVEL 18,000KM TO RAISE FUND

By a staff reporter

DUBAI — Sir Nicholas White, a Dubai resident, has begun a self-funded charity drive from Shanghai to London to raise money and awareness for two charities supporting those suffering from unnecessary blindness.

Having already travelled from Karachi to London by car some 38 years ago, Nick's original idea for the charity drive came from a BBC World programme about blindness hosted by former British prime minister John Major, which "struck a chord".

The 18,000km journey will see White navigate more than a dozen countries full of "scenic, cultural and historical locations on a journey that allows me to realise a life-long ambition of seeing Tibet and travelling the Silk Route," he said.

"The added plus is that I have been able to raise funds for Obis and Sight Savers, two charities that are endeavouring to restore the sight to many millions of people across the Third World through the Vision 2020 programme" — a worldwide initiative to eliminate unnecessary blindness launched by The World Health Organisation and The International Agency for Prevention of Blindness in 1999.

It is estimated that 1.5 million people go blind every year with 75 per cent of new cases preventable, or treatable in the very least.

Omnia, the Dubai Media City-based integrated marketing and design solution company, has donated a web site *www.18000kmtosavesight.org*, where visitors can check on White's progress kilometre-by-kilometre, relay messages of support, view picture updates of his incredible journey, read his daily blogs and most importantly, donate money to the cause.

"When White approached us detailing the severity of this global problem and how his ambitions lay in doing his bit for Vision 2020, we felt Omnia could lend a significant hand by becoming a sponsor and building and maintaining a dedicated web site detailing his trip" said Adam Booth, Managing Director, Omnia.

TRAVELLING FOR A CAUSE: Sir Nicholas White has begun a self-funded charity drive from Shanghai to London. — KT photo

Oriental Morning Post, Shanghai

[大都会] 上海启程 英国绅士驾车跨亚欧

早报记者 姚秋韵 责任编辑 方梅兰 2006-4-26 1:14:24

昨天下午，67岁的英国人尼古拉斯·怀特在上海的车辆交通管理部门顺利通过考核，拿到了中国境内的临时驾照，一旦他的红色沃尔沃SUV运抵中国，他就将开始自己的横跨亚欧的宏大之旅。按照怀特的计划，他将穿越中国、哈萨克斯坦、乌兹别克斯坦、俄罗斯、芬兰、挪威、瑞典、丹麦、德国、荷兰、比利时，终点是英国，全程18000公里。

上海翻译会陪到宜川

尼古拉斯·怀特原来是阿联酋FuturePipe集团的副总裁。2004年末，面临退休的他计划以驾车跨国旅行的方式回到自己的国家。

2005年2月，尼古拉斯提笔给中国政府写信，详细陈述了自己的意图并希望获得政府的批准。很快，国家旅游总局便以书信的形式给了他回复，不仅对于他的计划和寻求翻译帮助的设想表示同意，并委托国旅集团来配合他完成中国的行程。

经过近一年的准备，2006年4月20日，尼古拉斯从迪拜飞抵上海，边办理在中国境内必需的相关手续，边等待自己的心爱座驾运抵上海随时准备开始行程。国旅集团新上海国际旅行社的有关负责人表示，尼古拉斯在中国期间大致会有5到6个段陪翻译，其中上海国旅的翻译会陪同他到达宜川，与当地国旅的段陪完成交接。而一旦从新疆霍尔果斯边境办理完出境手续，接下来的行程将全部由尼古拉斯独自完成。

尼古拉斯在中国境内将停留的城市包括杭州、景德镇、武汉、宜川、重庆、成都、拉萨等，在穿越青藏高原，抵达拉萨之后，他将从敦煌开始进入悠远的丝绸之路。

为贫苦失明者筹款

原本只是单纯的退休旅行，但在2005年11月的某一天，当尼古拉斯收看了BBC关于慈善组织救治失明者的纪录片后，他决定在旅行计划中加入为慈善事业募捐的部分。

2005年圣诞节期间，尼古拉斯在英国与慈善治盲机构“OR－BIS”和“SIGHTSAVERS”代表见面并表达了要尽力为这些组织募集资金的想法。他希望募得善款可以用于在过去48年间他所工作过的国家，包括：尼泊尔、肯尼亚、坦桑尼亚、印度、巴基斯坦、阿联酋和中国。

通过早报呼吁募捐

昨天，奥比斯（ORBIS）中国区代表与尼古拉斯取得了联系，双方详谈了关于在中国境内的合作事宜。尼古拉斯说，他将会在旅行中拜访所有FuturePipe集团在中国境内的原料供应商，希望他们能够为慈善事业献出爱心。而奥比斯代表也表示，凡是在与奥比斯建立了合作关系的中国城市中，奥比斯会尽可能地为尼古拉斯提供帮助。

尼古拉斯同时通过东方早报向社会宣布，任何形式的捐助都不会与他本人发生接触，他所做的只是奔走相告，如果想要为失明者提供帮助，可以直接联系ORBIS中国上海办事处，通过登录ORBIS的中国网站或者尼古拉斯的个人网站（http://www.18000kmtosavesight.org/）了解其他详细情况。

尼古拉斯·怀特在上海的宾馆里等待出发。早报记者 鲁海涛图

Oriental Morning Post, Shanghai

(Translation)

[Metropolis] Shanghai set off for a British gentleman driving across Asia and Europe

Morning Post reporter Yao Qiuyun Editor in charge Fang Meilan 2006-4-26 1:14:24

Yesterday afternoon, Nicholas White, a 67-year-old British man, passed the assessment in Shanghai's vehicle traffic management department and obtained a temporary driver's license in China. Once his red Volvo SUV arrives in China, he will start his own journey across Asia and Europe. grand tour. According to White's plan, he will cross China, Kazakhstan, Uzbekistan, Russia, Finland, Norway, Sweden, Denmark, Germany, the Netherlands, Belgium, and the end point is the United Kingdom, a total distance of 18,000 kilometers.

Shanghai Interpreter Association accompanies Yichuan

Nicholas White was originally the Vice President of FuturePipe Group in the United Arab Emirates. In late 2004, facing retirement, he planned to travel back to his country by car.

In February 2005, Nicholas wrote a letter to the Chinese government, stating his intentions in detail and hoping to obtain government approval. Soon, the State Tourism Administration replied to him in the form of a letter, not only agreeing with his plan and the idea of seeking translation help, but also entrusting the China Travel Group to assist him in completing his China itinerary.

After nearly a year of preparation, Nicholas flew from Dubai to Shanghai on April 20, 2006. While going through the necessary procedures in China, he waited for his beloved car to arrive in Shanghai and was ready to start the journey. The relevant person in charge of the new Shanghai International Travel Service of CITS Group said that Nicholas will have 5 to 6 interpreters to accompany him during his stay in China. Among them, the interpreter of Shanghai International Travel Service will accompany him to Yichuan, and complete the handover with the local accompany of CITS. Once the exit formalities are completed from the Xinjiang Horgos border, the rest of the itinerary will be completed by Nicholas alone.

Nicholas will stop in cities in China including Hangzhou, Jingdezhen, Wuhan, Yichuan, Chongqing, Chengdu, Lhasa, etc. After crossing the Qinghai-Tibet Plateau and arriving in Lhasa, he will enter the distant Silk Road from Dunhuang.

Fundraising for the poor and blind

It was originally just a simple retirement trip, but one day in November 2005, when Nicholas watched a BBC documentary about a charity organization treating the blind, he decided to include a fundraising part in the travel plan.

During Christmas 2005, Nicholas met with representatives of charities "OR-BIS" and "SIGHTSAVERS" in the UK and expressed the idea of trying to raise funds for these organizations. He hopes the funds raised can be used in countries where he has worked for the past 48 years, including: Nepal, Kenya, Tanzania, India, Pakistan, UAE and China.

Call for donations through Morning Post

Yesterday, the representative of ORBIS in China got in touch with Nicholas, and the two sides discussed the cooperation in China in detail. Nicholas said that he will visit all the raw material suppliers of FuturePipe Group in China during the trip, hoping that they can donate love to charity. The representative of Orbis also said that in any Chinese city that has established a cooperative relationship with Orbis, Orbis will help Nicholas as much as possible.

At the same time, Nicholas announced to the society through the Oriental Morning Post that any form of donation will not contact him. Log on to ORBIS's Chinese website or Nicholas' personal website (http://www.18000kmtosavesight.org/) for other details.

Front wheels

white's world-wide wheels

by Sir Nick White

The 13,250 kilometres I've covered so far now appears significantly passed the half-way point, though an equally significant part of my journey is thanks to constant detours from my designated route for compulsory sight-seeing.

I'm approaching the start of week nine and am preparing to cross into Russia. I'm heading west and Europe is calling.

There have been numerous highlights and I've fulfiled a life-long ambition in seeing Tibet. The Summer Palace, built by the current exiled Dalai Lama and the Stuppas of the dead Dalai Lamas were extraordinary — an illustration of how wealth can come and go, like civilisations over the ages.

I will never forget seeing the Mogoa Caves in Dunhuang, which contained murals and statues of Buddha dating back to AD366, Crescent Spring, a natural oasis surrounded by 100ft-tall sand dunes with an 11th century pagoda in the centre, and the ancient cities of Gaochang and Jiaohe, which were destroyed by Tamerlane in the 14th century.

As I've headed west geographically, it has been amazing to see the demographic spread and religious diversity. The impact of Islam is increasingly evident, while the longevity of Buddhist beliefs in often ostracised communities is astounding.

The serenely beautiful, cascading mountain passes en route from China to Tibet were breathtaking. At more than 4,500 feet, I was grateful for the Volvo's traction on what were often terrible roads. The XC90 has been worth every penny.

Striking a formal pose at a reservoir 100km east of Tashkent

WEEK 8: Europe is calling although there is still a long way to go. We are near the capital of Uzbekistan but it feels time to reminisce already

To track Nick's progress or to donate, visit: www.18000kmtosavesight.org

omnia

Left:
Gulf News's "Wheels" section covering week 8 of the journey.

Front wheels

white's world-wide wheels

by Sir Nick White

Entering the European leg of my charity drive. I've covered almost 15,000km so far but have also been firmly hit with a case of pothole fever.

Leaving Kazakhstan and the Aral Sea, and nearing the border of the Russian Federation, the road quality rapidly deteriorated. Although the Volvo has generally navigated every crater I've hit along the way excellently, the burden of non-stop impacts has taken its toll, with two visits to the garage in a week.

That said, we are both still intact after the traumas of crossing into Russia from Uralsk. Just.

The first nightmare was the road to Aktobei, which was the most diabolical terrain I have yet encountered. The surface was so severely potholed, it resembled something lunar.

I damaged one shock absorber and had to have it repaired, so I decided to cut my losses and drive instead along the sand tracks running parallel to the 'road'. I knew the years of desert driving in Dubai would come in handy somewhere along my journey.

The second incident was on the road to the Saratov, crossing the Russia border. I hit a particularly large pothole and had to change the tyre to one with a smaller diameter. Unfortunately, the shock absorber was bent and the only way to continue was to visit to the local garage — or shack.

The service was excellent, though. I had the shock absorber straightened and they welded a piece of metal to strengthen it so I could continue on the road to Moscow.

The Volvo gets some first aid after a battering by Eurasian roads

WEEK 8: After no problems with the Volvo, I have to visit the garage twice as I enter the European leg of my charity drive, leaving Asia firmly behind

To track Nick's progress or to donate, visit: www.18000kmtosavesight.org

omnia

Left:
Gulf News's "Wheels" section covering the Kazakhstan shock absorber problems.

Right:
Gulf News's "Wheels" section covering week 9 of the journey.

Front *wheels*

white's world-wide wheels

by Sir Nick White

After the trials and tribulations of crossing Asia, I'm taking my time to enjoy the wonders of Russia. The fascinating history of this massive country leaves me spellbound – from the Mongul and Romanov eras, to the October Revolution, Soviet era and Cold War.

In Moscow, I visited the monument to Peter the Great near Gorky Park on the banks of the Moskva River. The 165ft monument features a strident Peter standing atop a frigate in full sail, brandishing a golden scroll — a tribute of immense magnitude.

Built by Ivan the Terrible to commemorate a successful military campaign against the Tartar Monguls, St Basil's Cathedral in Moscow's Red Square represents the beauty and beast in Russian history.

Finished in 1561, nine unique 'onion' domes adorn the cathedral's eloquent spires, each differently coloured and decorated in a breathtaking display of craft. Legend has it that upon completion of the church, the Tsar brutally ordered the architect, Postnik Yakovlev, to be blinded to prevent him from ever creating anything to rival its beauty.

Red Square itself is a wonder to behold. Images from my life flashed through my mind as I stood amid the crowds. Lenin's Mausoleum has to be one of Moscow's most curious tourist attractions.

To Muscovites, it's either a sombre reminder of a faded communist past, or a cherished relic of good times gone.

Still, for the wide-eyed tourist, it remains a must-see....

Moscow's stunning Red Square, with Lenin's Mausoleum behind

WEEK 9: Another host of spectacular sights, this time as we arrive in Moscow and marvel at Red Square and the curious Lenin Mausoleum

To track Nick's progress or to donate, visit: www.18000kmtosavesight.org

omnia

Front *wheels*

white's world-wide wheels

by Sir Nick White

The Russian experience is over. St Petersburg was a fantastic city for sight-seeing and I managed to brush up on my history — the only problem was fitting it all in.

The imperial capital must have more crystalline squares and glorious Cathedrals than any other city. St Isaac's and the Peter and Paul cathedrals were magnificent in their splendour.

However, the grandest of all was the Church of Resurrection — built on the spot where Emperor Alexander II was assassinated in 1881. The church is said to have more ornate mosaics than any other in Russia.

I also took in the statue of Alexsandr Pushkin, the 19th century author who is rightfully described as the founder of modern Russian literature and the country's greatest ever poet.

From Mother Russia, I crossed into Finland and travelled to Jyvaskyla — the roads were brand new and I made great time. The Volvo seems to be performing better and better as it nears its homeland.

The winding 222km drive from Oulu, made famous in the 18th/19th century as a pine-tar producer — a product used by ship builders to make hulls water tight, to Rovaniemi, a beautiful lakeside town, was the greenest leg of my journey yet.

This is Lapland, just 6km south of the Artic Circle, and I am not ashamed to admit I visited Santa's Paradise — a marketer's dream as one is simply drawn to it. You can send a Christmas card here and the facility keeps them until the appropriate time before sending them off to wherever around the world. Almost everyone has a white beard.

One of Russia's stunning cathedrals — and is that Sir Nick rollerskating?

WEEK 10: We continue to make good progress and leave Mother Russia behind for Santa's home, Lapland, heading for Volvo territory

To track Nick's progress or to donate, visit: www.18000kmtosavesight.org

omnia

Right:
Gulf News's "Wheels" section covering week 10 of the journey.

News

last

white's world-wide wheels

by Sir Nick White

I'm home! After 100 days of often gruelling travelling, I turned into my driveway and was welcomed home by a procession of my nearest and dearest family and friends. Judy, Rebecca and Nathalie, respectively of the Sightsavers and Orbis charities I'm supporting were also there.

With 26,750km on the clock, the route was considerably longer than the 18,000 I had envisioned — of which, a fair 5,000 can be attributed to my extra sight-seeing.

I must thank my brilliant guides for controlling and navigating my day-to-day routines and helping me squeeze in as many wonderful sights as possible. Gentlemen, you were brilliant.

The Volvo XC90 consumed 2,984 litres of petrol at an average cost of 91 cents a litre — although this figure was considerably lower before European prices took their toll. My sturdy horse performed impeccably and, aside from the shock absorber problem, I experienced no difficulties. Extremely comfortable and reliable, it allowed me to travel long distances at a time and still retain a level of freshness throughout. And, importantly for all those in Dubai, the air conditioning was great, despite taking a constant pummelling.

Amazingly, of my 92 travel days, I only suffered six days of rain, with four of these falling high in the Norwegian mountains. More impressively, I ate in restaurants and cafes everyday, trying the local food and drink on every occasion and not once did I fall foul to an upset stomach. The only thing I couldn't finish was the Yak-butter tea in Lhasa, Tibet. I won't be scouring the local supermarkets for that delicacy.

I hope the trip achieves as much for two such fine charities as it has for me. Raising awareness is one thing, raising money which can help reduce unnecessary blindness in the developing world is another, and far more crucial.

I've got a couple of weeks off now before flying back to Dubai on September 14th, coinciding with the visit of Orbis' Boeing 747 Flying Eye hospital to the emirate.

I would like to thank everyone I met for their hospitality and generosity, and the readers of **wheels** for keeping tabs on my journey.

To donate see www.18000km tosavesight.org

WEEK 14: Home to a party of friends and family, as well as Rebecca and Nathalie, of Sightsavers and Orbis, the charities which gain from my trip

Sir Nick back with his family in England — with 26,750km behind him

omnia

Right:
Gulf News's "Wheels" section covering the final stage of the journey.

Appendix 5

Tapestries Inspired By The Journey

I have always enjoyed tapestry, so I decided to have some bespoke tapestry canvases made from some of the photographs of my 2006 trip in China, which I then wove to create the finished tapestries..

On these pages are two examples of the details of the tapestries I have woven in the years since the journey. They depicting the Potala Palace in Lhasa, Tibet and the Great Buddha at Emei Mountain near Leshan in the Sichuan Province of China.

Above:
The Potala Palace in Lhasa, Tibet.

Opposite:
The Great Buddha at Leshan.

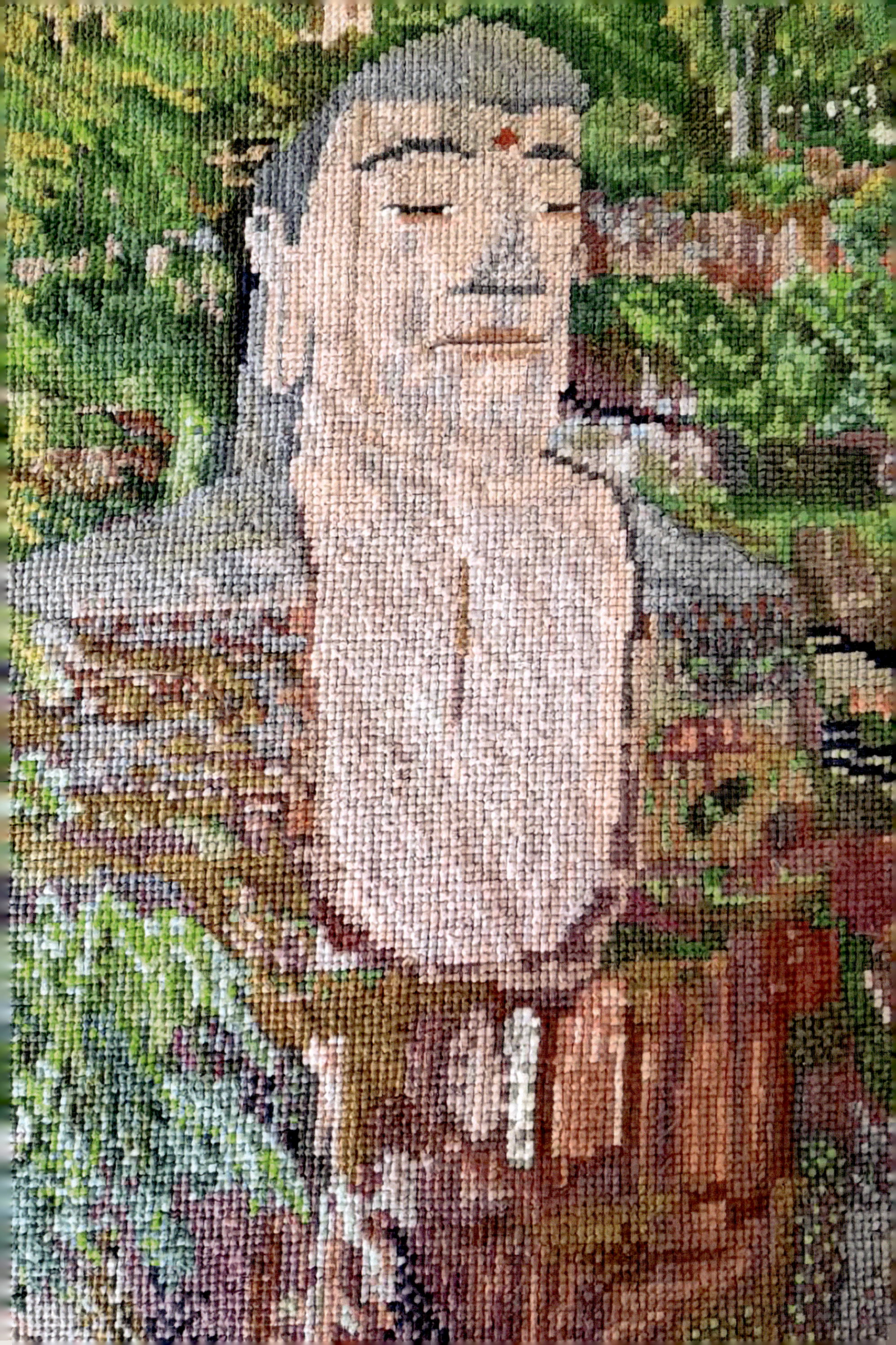

Appendix 6

The Route Map of My 1968 Journey

(see page 4)

Murmansk
Kola Peninsula
White Sea
Archangel
Vorkuta
Narvik
Bodø
Kiruna
Oulu
NORWAY
SWEDEN
FINLAND
Gulf of Bothnia
Trondheim
Kuopio
Pori
Tampere
Turku
Helsinki
Petrozavodsk
Bergen
Oslo
Uppsala
Stockholm
Tallinn
ESTONIA
St Petersburg
(Sankt-Peterburg)
Pskov
Yaroslavl
Nizhniy Novgorod
Kirov
Perm
Izhevsk
Kazan
Ural Mountains
Yekaterinburg
Kurgan
Chelyabinsk
Omsk
Tomsk
Novosibirsk
Surgut
Tobolsk
West Siberian Plain
RUS
DENMARK
Copenhagen
North Sea
Baltic Sea
Gotland
LATVIA
Riga
LITHUANIA
RUSSIA
Kaliningrad
Hamburg
NETH.
Amsterdam
Berlin
Poznań
Warsaw
(Warszawa)
Vilnius
Minsk
BELARUS
Moscow
(Moskva)
Smolensk
Tula
Ryazan
Ulyanovsk
Samara
Ufa
Orenburg
GERMANY
Cologne
Leipzig
POLAND
Brest
Voronezh
Saratov
Ural'sk
Aktobe
Astana
Pavlodar
Barnaul
Prague
Frankfurt
Stuttgart
Munich (München)
CZECH REP.
SLOVAKIA
Vienna
Bratislava
AUSTRIA
Budapest
HUNGARY
Kraków
Kiev (Kyiv)
L'viv
UKRAINE
Vinnytsya
Dnipropetrovs'k
Kharkiv
Luhans'k
Donets'k
Volgograd
Karaganda
KAZAKHSTAN
Ust' Kamenogorsk
Zürich
Bern
Ljubljana
Zagreb
MOLDOVA
Chişinău
Mariupol'
Rostov-na-Donu
Atyrau
Astrakhan
Milan
(Milano)
SLOV.
CROATIA
SERB.
ROMANIA
Odesa
Crimea
Sea of Azov
Krasnodar
Aral Sea
Lake Balkhash
Turin
Florence
(Firenze)
Sarajevo
BOS. and HERZ.
Belgrade
(Beograd)
Bucharest
(Bucureşti)
Constanta
Varna
Ustyurt Plateau
Corsica
Rome
(Roma)
MONT.
Prishtinë
BULGARIA
Sofia
Black Sea
Elbrus 5642
Groznyy
Caspian Sea
Kyzylkum
Shymkent
Bishkek
Almaty
Barcelona
Sardinia
Naples
(Napoli)
Podgorica
Tirana
ALBANIA
MACE.
Skopje
İstanbul
Samsun
GEORGIA
Tbilisi
AZERBAIJAN
ARMENIA
Yerevan
Baku
Toshkent
KYRGYZSTAN
UZBEKISTAN
TURKMENISTAN
Thessaloniki
Ankara
Bursa
TURKEY
Erzurum
Turkmenbaşy
Karakum Desert
Samarkand
TAJIKISTAN
Dushanbe
Mediterranean Sea
Ionian Sea
GREECE
Aegean Sea
İzmir
Konya
Gaziantep
Tabriz
Rasht
Aşgabat
Palermo
Sicily
Bizerte
Tunis
TUNISIA
Sousse
Sfax
Patras
Athens
Antalya
Adana
Aleppo
(Halab)
Mosul
Arbil
Elburz Mountains
Mashhad
Valletta
MALTA
Crete
Iraklion
Nicosia
CYPRUS
SYRIA
Tehrān
Herāt
Kābul
Peshawar
Tripoli
LEBANON
Beirut
Damascus
Baghdād
IRAN
Dasht-e Kavir
AFGHANISTAN
Rawalpindi
Islamabad
Banghāzī
Gulf of Sirte
ISRAEL
Jerusalem
Amman
JORDAN
IRAQ
Esfahān
Kandahār
Amritsar
Alexandria
(Al Iskandarīyah)
An Najaf
Ahvāz
Basra
KUWAIT
Kuwait
Kerman
Quetta
Lahore
Multan
Ludhiana
Chandigarh
LIBYA
EGYPT
Cairo
(Al Qāhirah)
Suez
Nafud
Shiraz
Bushehr
Zahedan
PAKISTAN
Baluchistan
Delhi
NEPAL
Libyan Desert
SAUDI
The Gulf
Bandar-e-'Abbās
Jaipur
Agra
Kathmandu
Lucknow
Asyūţ
BAHRAIN
Manama
QATAR
Doha
Dubai
(Dubayy)
Jodhpur
Gwalior
Aswān
Red Sea
Riyadh
(Ar Riyad)
U.A.E.
Abu Dhabi
Gulf of Oman
Karachi
Hyderabad
Rann of Kutch
Allahabad
Ghat
Sahara
ARABIA
Muscat
(Masqat)
Ahmadabad
Jabalpur
Indore
Ranchi
Jeddah (Jiddah)
OMAN
Surat
Nagpur
Rub' al Khali
Nashik
INDIA
Tibesti
Port Sudan
Mumbai
Pune
Hyderabad
NIGER
CHAD
ERITREA
YEMEN
Salalah
Khartoum
Massawa
San'a'
Asmara
Hodeidah
Mukalla (Al Mukalla)
Arabian Sea
Panaji
Vijayawada
Zinder
SUDAN
Ras Dejen 4533
Aden (Adan)
Socotra
Bangalore
Chennai
Kano
Ndjamena
El Obeid
DJIBOUTI
Djibouti
Gulf of Aden
Mangalore
Mysore
Calicut
Tiruchirapalli
NIGERIA
Abuja
Sarh
Addis Ababa
(Adis Abeba)
Berbera
Somaliland
Laccadive Is.
(India)
Ogbomosho
Ibadan
Lagos
Onitsha
CENTRAL AFRICAN REPUBLIC
Bangui
Bossangoa
Ngaoundéré
CAMEROON
Douala
Yaoundé
SOUTH SUDAN
Wau
Juba
ETHIOPIA
Dire Dawa
SOMALIA
Thiruvananthapuram
Jaffna
Sri Jayewardenepura Kotte
Colombo
Kandy
SRI LANKA
Malabo
DEMOCRATIC REPUBLIC OF THE CONGO
EQUAT. GUINEA
Libreville
GABON
CONGO
Kisangani
UGANDA
Kampala
L. Turkana
KENYA
Mount Kenya
Nakuru
Nairobi
Mogadishu
(Muqdisho)
Kismayu
MALDIVES
Male
Port Gentil
Mbandaka
Kigali
RWANDA
Bujumbura
BURUNDI
Mwanza
Kilimanjaro
Arusha
Mombasa
SEYCHELLES
Victoria
Praslin
Mahé
Gan
Addu Atoll
Brazzaville
Pointe Noire
CABINDA
Kinshasa
Kananga
Tabora
Tanga
TANZANIA
Dodoma
Pemba
Zanzibar
Dar es Salaam
Amirante Islands
Desroches
Salomon Is.
Chagos Archipelago
British Indian Ocean Terr.
(U.K.)
Diego Garcia
Luanda
Kolwezi
Mbeya
Kilwa Masoko
Mtwara
Aldabra Is.
Farquhar Group
Coëtivy
ANGOLA
Benguela
Huambo
Lubumbashi
ZAMBIA
Kitwe
MALAWI
Lilongwe
Lake Nyasa
COMOROS
Moroni
Mayotte
(Fr.)
Antseranana
Agalega Is.
(Maur.)
INDIA
Namibe
Lubango
Lusaka
Lichinga
MOZAMBIQUE
Nampula
Mahajanga
Tsaratanana 2876
Harare
ZIMBABWE
Bulawayo
Blantyre
Quelimane
Mozambique Channel
Toamasina
Antananarivo
MADAGASCAR
Île Tromelin
(Fr.)
Cargados Carajos Islands
(Maur.)
NAMIBIA
Beira
Bassas da India
(Fr.)
Port Louis
MAURITIUS
Rodrigues
(Maur.)
Swakopmund
Walvis Bay
Windhoek
BOTSWANA
Europa
Fianarantsoa
Réunion
(Fr.)

Made in the USA
Monee, IL
14 April 2022

e30dcf42-9249-43ee-9875-c2c47241ff78R02